DEAN SWIFT.

IRISH WIT AND HUMOR.

ANECDOTE BIOGRAPHY

OF

SWIFT, CURRAN, O'LEARY

AND O'CONNELL.

NEW YORK:
J. A. McGEE, 9 BARCLAY STREET.
1872.

Stereotyped at the New York Catholic Protectory,
West Chester, N. Y.

CONTENTS.

DEAN SWIFT.

JOHN PHILPOT CURRAN.

ARTHUR O'LEARY.

DANIEL O'CONNELL.

IRISH WIT AND HUMOR.

DEAN SWIFT.

HIS BIRTH.

Dr. Jonathan Swift, Dean of St. Patrick's, was born A.D. 1667, in Hoey's Court, Dublin, the fourth house, right hand side, as you enter from Werburgh-street. The houses in this court still bear evidence of having been erected for the residence of respectable folks. The "Dean's House," as it is usually designated, had marble chimney-pieces, was wainscotted from hall to garret, and had panelled oak doors, one of which is in possession of Doctor Willis, Rathmines—a gentleman who takes a deep interest in all matters connected with the history of his native city.

SINGULAR EVENT.

When Swift was a year old, an event happened to him that seems very unusual; for his nurse, who was a woman of Whitehaven, being under the absolute necessity of seeing one of her relations, who was then extremely sick, and from whom she expected a legacy; and being extremely fond of the infant, she stole him on shipboard unknown to his mother and uncle, and carried him with her to Whitehaven, where he continued for almost three years. For, when the matter was discovered, his mother sent orders by all means not to hazard a second voyage till he could be better able to bear it. The nurse was so careful of him that before he returned he had learned to spell; and by the time that he was five years old, he could read any chapter in the Bible.

After his return to Ireland he was sent at six years old to the school of Kilkenny, from whence at fourteen he was admitted into the Dublin University.

A CERTIFICATE OF MARRIAGE.

Swift, in one of his pedestrian journeys from London towards Chester, is reported to have taken shelter from a summer tempest under a large oak on the road side, at no great distance from Litchfield. Presently, a man, with a pregnant woman, were driven by the like impulse to avail themselves of the same covert. The Dean, entering into conversation, found the parties were destined for Litchfield to be married. As the situation of the woman indicated no time should be lost, a proposition was made on his part to save them the rest of the journey, by performing the ceremony on the spot. The offer was gladly accepted, and thanks being duly returned, the bridal pair, as the sky brightened, was about to return: but the bridegroom suddenly recollecting that a certificate was requisite to authenticate the marriage, requested one, which the Dean wrote in these words:

Under an oak, in stormy weather,
I joined this rogue and wench together,
And none but he who rules the thunder,
Can put this wench and rogue asunder.

GRACE AFTER DINNER.

Swift was once invited by a rich miser with a large party to dine; being requested by the host to return thanks at the removal of the cloth, uttered the following grace:—

Thanks for this miracle!—this is no less
Than to eat manna in the wilderness.
Where raging hunger reign'd we've found relief,

And seen that wondrous thing, a piece of beef.
Here chimneys smoke, that never smok'd before,
And we've all ate, where we shall eat no more!

THE THREE CROSSES.

Swift in his journeys on foot from Dublin to London, was accustomed to stop for refreshments or rest at the neat little ale-houses at the road's side. One of these, between Dunchurch and Daventry, was formerly distinguished by the sign of the *Three Crosses,* in reference to the three intersecting ways which fixed the site of the house. At this the Dean called for his breakfast, but the landlady, being engaged with accommodating her more constant customers, some wagoners, and staying to settle an altercation which unexpectedly arose, keeping him waiting, and inattentive to his repeated exclamations, he took from his pocket a diamond, and wrote on every pane of glass in her best room:—

TO THE LANDLORD.

There hang three crosses at thy door:
Hang up thy wife, and she'll make four.

CHIEF JUSTICE WHITSHED.

Swift, in a letter to Pope, thus mentions the conduct of this worthy Chief Justice:—

"I have written in this kingdom a discourse to persuade the wretched people to wear their own manufactures instead of those from England: this treatise soon spread very fast, being agreeable to the sentiments of a whole nation, except of those gentlemen who had employments, or were expectants. Upon which a person in great office here immediately took the alarm; he sent in haste to Lord Chief Justice Whitshed, and informed him of a seditious, factious, and virulent pamphlet, lately published, with a design of setting the two kingdoms at variance, directing at the same time that the printer should be prosecuted with the utmost rigor of the law. The Chief Justice had so quick an understanding that he resolved, if possible, to outdo his orders. The grand juries of the county and city were practised effectually with to represent the said pamphlet with all aggravating epithets, for which they had thanks sent them from England, and their presentments published for several weeks in all the newspapers. The printer was seized, and forced to give great bail: after this trial the jury brought him in *not guilty*, although they had been culled with the greatest industry. The Chief Justice sent them back nine times, and kept them eleven hours, until, being tired out, they were forced to leave the matter to the mercy of the judge, by what they call a special verdict. During the trial, the Chief Justice, among other singularities, laid his hand on his breast, and protested solemnly that the author's design was to bring in the Pretender, although there was not a single syllable of party in the whole treatise, and although it was known that the most eminent of those who professed his own principles publicly disallowed his proceedings. But the cause being so very odious and unpopular, the trial of the verdict was deferred from one term to another, until, upon the arrival of the Duke of Grafton, the Lord Lieutenant, his Grace, after mature advice and permission from England, was pleased to grant a *nolle prosequi.*"

CHIEF JUSTICE WHITSHED'S MOTTO ON HIS COACH.

Libertas et natale solum.
Liberty and my native country.

Libertas et natale solum;
Fine words! I wonder where you stole 'em:
Could nothing but thy chief reproach
Serve for a motto on thy coach?

But let me now the words translate:
Natale solum :—my estate:
My dear estate, how well I love it!
My tenants, if you doubt, will prove it.
They swear I am so kind and good,
I hug them till I squeeze their blood.
Libertas bears a large import:
First, how to swagger in a court;
And, secondly, to show my fury
Against an uncomplying Jury;
And, thirdly, 'tis a new invention
To favor Wood, and keep my pension:
And fourthly, 'tis to play an odd trick,
Get the Great Seal, and turn out *Brod'rick.*
And, fifthly, you know whom I mean,
To humble that vexatious Dean;
And, sixthly, for my soul to barter it
For fifty times its worth to Carteret.
Now since your motto thus you construe,
I must confess you've spoken once true.
Libertas et natale solum,
You had good reason when you stole 'em.

ON THE SAME UPRIGHT CHIEF JUSTICE WHITSHED.

In church your grandsire cut his throat:
To do the job too long he tarried,
He should have had my hearty vote,
To cut his throat before he married.

TO QUILCA.

This was a country house of Dr. Sheridan's, where Swift and some of his friends spent a summer in the year 1725, and being in very bad repair, Swift wrote the following lines on the occasion:—

Let me thy properties explain :
A rotten cabin dropping rain :
Chimneys with scorn rejecting smoke :
Stools, tables, chairs and bedsteads broke.
Here elements have lost their uses,
Air ripens not, nor earth produces :
In vain we make poor Shelah toil,
Fire will not roast, nor water boil.
Through all the valleys, hills, and plains,
The *goddess Want* in triumph reigns ;
And her chief officers of state ;
Sloth, Dirt, and Theft, around her wait.

MR. PULTENEY.

Swift says, in a letter to Mr. Pulteney: "I will do an unmannerly thing, which is to bequeath you an epitaph for forty years hence, in two words, *ultimus Britannorum.* You never forsook your party. You might often have been as great as the court can make any man so ; but you preserved your spirit of liberty when your former colleagues had utterly sacrificed theirs; and if it shall ever begin to breathe in these days, it must entirely be owing to yourself and one or two friends; but it is altogether impossible for any nation to preserve its liberty long under a tenth part of the present luxury, infidelity, and a million of corruptions. We see the Gothic system of limited monarchy is extinguished in all the nations of Europe. It is utterly extirpated in this wretched kingdom, and yours must be next. Such has ever been human nature, that a single man, without any superior advantages either of body or mind, but usually the direct contrary, is able to attach twenty millions, and drag them voluntarily at his chariot wheels. But no more of this: I am as sick of the world as I am of age and disease. I live in a nation of slaves, who sell themselves for nothing."

RESOLUTIONS WHEN I COME TO BE OLD.

These resolutions seem to be of that kind which are easily formed, and the propriety of which we readily admit at the time we make them, but secretly never design to put them in practice.

1. Not to marry a young woman.

2. Not to keep young company, unless they really desire it.

3. Not to be peevish, or morose, or suspicious.

4. Not to scorn present ways, or wits, or fashions, or men, or war, &c.

5. Not to be fond of children.

6. Not to tell the same story over and over to the same people.

7. Not to be covetous.

8. Not to neglect decency or cleanliness, for fear of falling into nastiness.

9. Not to be over severe with young people, but to give allowance for their youthful follies and weaknesses.

10. Not to be influenced by, or give ear to, knavish tattling servants, or others.

11. Not to be too free of advice, nor trouble any but those who desire it.

12. To desire some good friends to inform me which of these resolutions I break or neglect, and wherein; and reform accordingly.

13. Not to talk much, nor of myself.

14. Not to boast of my former beauty or favor with ladies, &c.

15. Not to hearken to flatteries, or believe I can be beloved by a young woman.

16. Not to be positive or opiniative.

17. Not to set up for observing all these rules, for fear I should observe none.

MISS BENNET.

This lady was a celebrated beauty in her day, and often mentioned by Swift. Dr. Arbuthnot thus speaks of her in one of his letters: "Amongst other things, I had the honor to carry an Irish lady to court that was admired beyond all the ladies in France for her beauty. She had great honors done her. The hussar himself was ordered to bring her the King's cat to kiss. Her name is Bennet."

This circumstance gave rise to the following lines by the Dean:—

For when as Nelly came to France,
(Invited by her cousins)
Across the *Tuileries* each glance
Kill'd Frenchmen by whole dozens.

The king, as he at dinner sat,
Did beckon to his hussar,
And bid him bring his tabby cat
For charming Nell to buss her.

The ladies were with rage provok'd,
To see her so respected;
The men look'd arch as Nelly strok'd,
And puss her tail erected.

But not a man did look employ,
Except on pretty Nelly;
Then said the Duke de Villeroi,
Ah! *qu'elle est bien jolie!*

The courtiers all with one accord,
Broke out in Nelly's praises:
Admir'd her rose, and *lis sans farde,*
Which are your terms *Francaises.*

THE FEAST OF O'ROURKE.

Swift had been heard to say more than once that he should like to pass a few days in the county of Leitrim, as he was told that the native Irish in that part were so obstinately attached to the rude manners of their ancestors, that they could neither be induced by *promises*, nor forced by *threats*, to exchange them for those of their neighbors. Swift, no doubt, wished to know what they would get by the exchange. Mr. Core was resolved that the Dean should be indulged to the fullest extent of his wish; for this purpose he had a person posted in Cavan, who was to give him immediate notice when the Dean arrived in that town, which he usually did once a year, and where he remained a day or two or longer, if the weather was not fair enough to travel. The instant Mr.

Gore was informed of the Dean's arrival, he called and invited him to pass a few days at a noble mansion which he had just finished on a wing of his own estate in that county. The Dean accepted the invitation; and, as the season was fine, every thing as he advanced excited his attention; for, like other men, he was at times subject to "the skyey influence," and used to complain of the winds of March, and the gloom of November.

Mr. Gore had heard so much of Swift's peculiar manners that he was determined he should have his way in every thing; but was resolved, however, that he should be entertained in the old Irish style of hospitality, which Mr. Gore always kept up to such a degree, that his house might be called a public inn without sign. The best pipers and harpers were collected from every quarter, as well as the first singers, for music is an essential ingredient in every Irish feast. The Dean was pleased with many of the Irish airs, but was peculiarly struck with the Feast of O'Rourke, which was played by Jeremy Dignum, the Irish Timotheus, who swept the lyre with flying fingers, when he was told that in the judgment of the Dean, he carried off the *spolia opima* from all the rest of the musical circle. The words of the air were afterwards sung by a young man with so much taste and execution, that the Dean expressed a desire to have them translated into English. Dr. Gore told him that the author, a Mr. Macgowran, lived at a little distance, and that he would be proud to furnish a literal translation of his own composition either in Latin or English, for he was well skilled in both languages. Mr. Gore accordingly sent for the bard, the Laureate of the Plains, as he called himself, who came immediately. "I am very well pleased," said the Dean, "with your composition. The words seem to be what my friend Pope calls 'an echo to the sense.'" "I am pleased and proud," answered Macgowran, "that it has afforded you any amusement: and when you, Sir," addressing himself to the Dean, "put all the strings of the Irish harp in tune, it will yield your Reverence a double pleasure, and perhaps put me out of my senses with joy." Macgowran, in a short time, presented the Dean with a literal translation, for which he rewarded him very liberally, and recommended him to the protection of Mr. Gore, who behaved with great kindness to him as long as he lived. To this incident we are indebted for the translation of a song or poem, which may be called a true picture of an Irish feast, where every one was welcome to eat what he pleased, to drink what he pleased, to say what he pleased, to sing what he pleased, to fight when he pleased, to sleep when he pleased, and to dream what he pleased; where all was native—their dress the produce of their own shuttle—their cups and tables the growth of their own woods—their whiskey *warm from the still and faithful to its fires!* The Dean, however, did not translate the whole of the poem; the remaining stanzas were translated some years since by Mr. Wilson, as follow:—

Who rais'd this alarm?
  Says one of the clergy,
And threat'ning severely,
  Cease fighting, I charge ye.

A good knotted staff,
  The full of his hand,
Instead of the *Spiradis*,
  Back'd his command.

So falling to thrash,
  Fast as he was able,
A trip and a box
  Stretch'd him under the table.

Then rose a big friar,
  To settle them straight,
But the back of the fire
  Was quickly his fate.

From whence he cried out,
  Do you thus treat your *pastors!*
Ye that scarcely were bred
  To the *seven wise masters;*

That when with the Pope
  I was getting my lore,
Ye were roasting potatoes
  At the foot of *Sheemor.*

SWIFT'S BEHAVIOR AT TABLE.

Swift's manner of entertaining his guests, and his behavior at table, were curious. A frequent visitor thus described them: He placed himself at the head of the table, and opposite to a great pier glass, so that he could see whatever his servants did at the marble side-board behind his chair. He was served entirely in plate, and with great elegance. The beef being once over-roasted, he called for the cook-maid to take it down stairs and do it less. The girl very innocently replied that she could not. "Why, what sort of a creature are you," exclaimed he, "to commit a fault which cannot be mended?" Then, turning to one that sate next to him, he said very gravely, that he hoped, as the cook was a woman of genius, he should, by this manner of arguing, be able, in about a year's time, to convince her she had better send up the meat too little than too much done: at the same time he charged the men-servants, that whenever they thought the meat was ready, to take it up, spit and all, and bring it up by force, promising to assist them in case the cook resisted. Another time the Dean turning his eye towards the looking-glass, espied the butler opening a bottle of ale, and helping himself. "Ha, friend," said the Dean, "sharp is the word with you, I find: you have drunk my ale, for which I stop two shillings out of your board wages this week, for I scorn to be outdone in any thing, even in cheating."

COUNTESS OF BURLINGTON.

Swift was dining one day with the Earl of Burlington soon after his lordship's marriage, when that nobleman, expecting some diversion from Swift's oddities of behavior, purposely neglected to name him to his lady, who was entirely ignorant of the Dean's person. The Dean generally wore his gowns till they were quite rusty, which being the case, she supposed him to be some clergyman of no great consequence. After dinner, the Dean said to her, "Lady Burlington, I hear you can sing; come, sing me a song." The Lady, disgusted with this unceremonious way of asking such a favor, positively refused him. He said she could sing, or he would make her. "What, madam, I suppose you take me for one of your poor paltry English hedge-parsons; sing, when I bid you!" As the Earl did nothing but laugh at his freedom, the lady was so vexed that she burst into tears, and retired. His first compliment when he saw her a little time afterwards was, "Pray, madam, are you as proud and ill-natured now as when I saw you last?" To which she replied with the greatest good humor, "No, Mr. Dean; I will sing for you now, if you please." From this time he conceived the greatest esteem for her, and always behaved with the utmost respect. Those who knew Swift, took no offence at his bluntness of behavior. It seems Queen Caroline did not, if we may credit his words in the verses on his own death.

SWIFT'S POLITICAL PRINCIPLES.

In a letter to Pope, alluding to the days when he took part in politics, he thus expresses himself:—

"I had likewise in those days a mortal antipathy to standing armies in times of peace. Because I always took standing armies to be only servants, hired by the master of the family to keep his own children in slavery; and because I conceived that a prince who could not think himself secure wit hout mercenary troops, must needs have a separate interest from that of his subjects.

"As to Parliaments, I adored the wisdom of that Gothic institution which made them annual, and I was confident that our liberty could never be placed upon a firm foundation until that ancient law were restored among us. For who sees not, that while such assemblies are permitted to have a longer duration, there grows up a commerce of corruption between the ministry and the deputies, wherein they both find account, to the manifest danger of liberty; which traffic would neither answer the design nor expense, if parliaments met once a year.

"I ever abominated that scheme of politics (now about thirty years old) of setting up a moneyed interest in opposition to that of the landed: for I conceived there could not be a truer maxim in goverment than this, that the possessors of the soil are the best judges of what is for the advantage of the kingdom. If others had thought the same way, funds of credit and South Sea projects would neither have been felt nor heard of.

"I could never see the necessity of *suspending any law* upon which the liberty of the most innocent persons depend: neither do I think this practice has made the taste of arbitary power so agreeable as that we should desire to see it repeated. Every rebellion subdued, and plot discovered, contributes to the firmer establishment of the Prince: in the latter case, the knot of conspirators is entirely broken, and they are to begin their work anew under a thousand disadvantages; so that those diligent inquiries into remote and problematical guilt, with a new power of enforcing them by chains and dungeons to every person whose face a minister thinks fit to dislike, are not only opposite to that maxim which declares it better that ten guilty men should escape than one innocent suffer, but likewise leave a gate wide open to the whole tribe of informers, the most accursed, and prostitute, and abandoned race that God ever permitted to plague mankind."

SWIFT'S CHARITY.

One cold morning a poor ancient woman sat at the deanery steps a considerable time, during which the dean saw her through a window, and, no doubt, commiserated her desolate condition. His footman happened to go to the door, and the poor creature besought him to give a paper to his reverence. The servant read it, and told her his master had something else to do than to mind her petition. "What is that you say, fellow?" said the dean, putting his head out of the window; "come up here directly." The man obeyed him, and was ordered to tell the woman to come up to him. After bidding her to be seated, he directed some bread and wine to be given to her; after which, turning round to the man, he said, "At what time did I order you to open and read a paper directed to me? or to refuse a letter from any one? Hark you, sirrah, you have been admonished by me for drunkenness, idleness, and other faults; but since I have discovered your inhuman disposition, I must dismiss you from my service: so pull off your clothes, take your wages, and let me hear no more of you."

PUBLIC ABSURDITIES IN IRELAND.

Among the public absurdities in Ireland, Swift notices the insurance office against fire; the profits of which to the amount of several thousand pounds, were annually remitted to England. "For," observes he, "as if we could well spare the money, the society-marks upon our houses spread faster and further than the colony of frogs; and we are not only indebted to England for the materials to light our own fires, but for engines to put them out."

SWIFT'S PECULIARITY OF HUMOR.

Trifles become of some consequence when connected with a great name, or when they throw any light on a distinguished character. Spence thus relates a story told by Pope: "Dr. Swift had an odd blunt way that is mistaken by strangers for ill nature. It is so odd that there is no describing it but by facts. I'll tell you one that first comes into my head. One evening Gay and I went to see him: you know how intimately we were all acquainted. On our coming in, "Hey-day, gentlemen (says the Doctor), what's the meaning of this visit? How came you to leave all the Lords that you are so fond of, to come here to see a poor Dean?" "Because we would rather see you than any of them." "Ay, any one that did not know you so well as I do, might believe you. But since you are come, I must get some supper for you, I suppose." "No, Doctor, we have supped already." "Supped already, that's impossible! why it is not eight o'clock yet. That's very strange! But, if you had not supped, I must have got something for you. Let me see what should I have had? A couple of lobsters; ay, that would have done very well; two shillings: tarts, a shilling. But you will drink a glass of wine with me, though you supped so much before your usual time only to spare my pocket." "No, we had rather talk with you than drink with you." "But if you had supped with me, as in all reason you ought to have done, you must then have drank with me.

A bottle of wine, two shillings—two and two is four, and one is five; just two and sixpence a piece. There, Pope, there's half-a-crown for you; and there's another for you, Sir; for I won't save any thing by you, I am determined.' This was all said and done with his usual seriousness on such occasions; and in spite of every thing we could say to the contrary, he actually obliged us to take the money."

DR. BOLTON.

Dr. Theophilus Bolton was not only a learned divine, but a very fine gentleman. His merit as a preacher was so eminent that it was early rewarded with a mitre. Swift went to congratulate him on the occasion, when he observed that as his lordship was a native of Ireland, and had now a seat in the House of Peers, he hoped he would employ his eloquence in the service of his distressed country. The prelate told him the bishopric was but a very small one, and he could not hope for a better if he disobliged the court. "Very well," said Swift; "then it is to be hoped when you have a better you will become an honest man." "Ay, that I will, Mr. Dean." "Till then, my lord, farewell," answered Swift. The prelate was soon translated to a richer see, on which occasion Swift called to remind him of his promise; but to no purpose: there was an archbishopric in view, and till that was obtained nothing could be done. Having in a few years attained this object likewise, he then waited on the Dean, and told him, "I am now at the top of my preferment, for I well know that no Irishman will ever be made primate; therefore, as I can rise no higher in fortune or station, I will most zealously promote the good of my country." From that he became a most active patriot.

THE SCRIBLERUS CLUB.

Before Swift retired to Ireland, Mr. Pope, Dr. Arbuthnot, Mr. Gay, Mr. Parnell, Mr. Jervas, and Swift formed themselves into a society called the Scriblerus Club. They wrote a good many things in conjunction, and, according to Goldsmith, Gay was usually the amanuensis. The connection between these wits advanced the fame and interest of them all. They submitted their several productions to the review of their friends, and readily adopted alterations dictated by taste and judgment, unmixed with envy, or any sinister motive.

When the members of the Scriblerus Club were in town, they were generally together, and often made excursions into the country. They generally preferred walking to riding, and all agreed once to walk down to Lord Burlington's about twelve miles from town. It was Swift's custom in whatever company he might visit to travel, to endeavor to procure the best bed for himself. To secure that, on the present occasion, Swift, who was an excellent walker, proposed, as they were leaving town, that each should make the best of his way. Dr. Parnell, guessing the Dean's intentions, pretended to agree; but as his friend was out of sight, he took a horse, and arrived at his Lordship's by another way, before Swift. Having acquainted his noble host with the other's design, he begged of him to disappoint it. It was resolved that Swift should be kept out of the house. Swift had never had the small-pox, and was, as all his friends knew, very much afraid of catching that distemper. A servant was despatched to meet him as he was approaching the gate, and to tell him that the small-pox was raging in the house, that it would be unsafe for him to enter the doors, but that there was a field-bed in the summer house in the garden, at his service. Thither the Dean was under the necessity of betaking himself. He was forced to be content with a cold supper, whilst his friends, whom he had tried to outstrip, were feasting in the house. At last after they thought they had sufficiently punished his too eager desire for his own accommodation, they requested his lordship to admit him into the company. The Dean was obliged to promise he would not afterwards, when with his friends, attempt to secure the best bed to himself. Swift was often the butt of their waggery, which he bore with great good humor, knowing well, that though they laughed at his singularities, they esteemed his virtues, admired his wit, and venerated his wisdom.

Many were the frolics of the Scriblerus Club. They often evinced the truth of an observation made by the poet, "*dulce est desipere in loco.*"

The time for wits to play the fool, is when they are met together, to relax from the severity of mental exertion. Their follies have a degree of extravagance much beyond the phlegmatic merriment of sober dulness, and can be relished by those only, who having wit themselves, can trace the extravagance to the real source.

This society carefully abstained from their frolics before the stupid and ignorant, knowing that on no occasion ought a wise man to guard his words and actions more than when in the company of fools.

How long the Scriblerus Club lasted is not exactly ascertained, or whether it existed during the intimacy between Swift and Addison, previous to the Doctor's connection with the Tory ministry.

THE UPSTART.

There was one character which, through life, always kindled Swift's indignation, *the haughty, presuming, tyrannizing upstart!* A person of this description chanced to reside in the parish of Laracor. Swift omitted no opportunity of humbling his pride; but, as he was as ignorant as insolent, he was obliged to accommodate the coarseness of the lash to the callosity of the back. The following lines have been found written by Swift upon this man:—

The rascal! that's too mild a name;
Does he forget from whence he came;
Has he forgot from whence he sprung;
A mushroom in a bed of dung;
A maggot in a cake of fat,
The offspring of a beggar's brat.
As eels delight to creep in mud,
To eels we may compare his blood;
His blood in mud delights to run;
Witness his lazy, lousy son!
Puff'd up with pride and insolence,
Without a grain of common sense,
See with what consequence he stalks,
With what pompósity he talks;
See how the gaping crowd admire
The stupid blockhead and the liar.
How long shall vice triumphant reign?
How long shall mortals bend to gain?
How long shall virtue hide her face,
And leave her votaries in disgrace?
—Let indignation fire my strains,
Another villain yet remains—
Let purse-proud C——n next approach,
With what an air he mounts his coach!
A cart would best become the knave,
A dirty parasite and slave;
His heart in poison deeply dipt,
His tongue with oily accents tipt,
A smile still ready at command,
The pliant bow, the forehead bland—

MEDITATION UPON A BROOMSTICK.

This single stick, which you now behold ingloriously lying in that neglected corner, I once knew in a flourishing state in a forest; it was full of sap, full of leaves, and full of boughs: but now in vain does the busy art of man pretend to vie with nature, by tying that withered bundle of twigs to its sapless trunk. It is now at best but the reverse of what it was, a tree turned upside down, the branches on the earth, and the root in the air. It is now handled by every dirty wench, condemned to do her drudgery, and by a capricious kind of fate, destined to make her things clean, and be nasty itself. At length, worn out to the stumps in the service of the maids, it is either thrown out of doors, or condemned to the last use, of kindling a fire. When I beheld this, I sighed and said within myself, *Surely, mortal man is a broomstick!* Nature sent him into the world strong and lusty, in a thriving condition, wearing his own hair on his head, the proper branches of this reasoning vegetable, until the axe of intemperance has lopped off his green boughs, and left him a withered trunk: he then flies to art, and puts on a periwig, valuing himself upon an unnatural bundle of hairs, all covered with powder, that never grew upon his head; but now, should this, *our broomstick*, pretend to enter the scene, proud of those birchen spoils it never bore, and all covered with dust, though the sweepings of the finest lady's chamber, we should be apt to ridicule and despise its vanity. Partial judges that we are of our own excellencies, and other men's defaults!

But a *broomstick*, perhaps you will say, is an emblem of a tree standing on its head; and pray what is man but a topsy-turvy creature, his animal faculties perpetually mounted on his rational, his head where his heels should be, groveling on the earth! and yet, with all his faults, he sets up to be a universal reformer and corrector of abuses, a remover of grievances, * * sharing deeply all the while in the very same pollutions he pretends to sweep away: his last days are spent in slavery to women, and generally the least deserving; till worn to the stumps like his brother besom, he is either kicked out of doors, or made use of to kindle flames for others to warm themselves by.

COSSING A DOG.

In a humorous paper written in 1732, entitled, "An Examination of certain Abuses, Corruptions, and Enormities in the city of Dublin," Swift mentions this diversion, which he ludicrously enough applies to the violent persecutions of the political parties of the day. The ceremony was this: A strange dog happens to pass through a flesh market; whereupon an expert butcher immediately cries in a loud voice and proper tone, *coss*, *coss*, several times. The same word is repeated by the people. The dog, who perfectly understands the terms of art, and consequently the danger he is in, immediately flies. The people, and even his own brother animals, pursue: the pursuit and cry attend him perhaps half a mile; he is well worried in his flight; and sometimes hardly escapes. "This," adds Swift, "our ill-wishers of the Jacobite kind are pleased to call a persecution; and affirm, that it always falls upon dogs of the *Tory* principles."

TRADE OF IRELAND.

Swift being one day at a sheriff's feast, among other toasts the chairman called out, "Mr. Dean, the Trade of Ireland." The Dean answered, "Sir, *I drink no memories.*" The idea of the answer was evidently taken from Bishop Brown's book against "Drinking the Memories of the dead," which had just then appeared, and made much noise.

A BEGGAR'S WEDDING.

As Swift was fond of scenes in low life, he missed no opportunity of being present at them when they fell in his way. Once when he was in the country, he received intelligence that there was to be a beggar's wedding in the neighborhood. He was resolved not to miss the opportunity of seeing so curious a ceremony; and that he might enjoy the whole completely, proposed to Dr. Sheridan that he should go thither disguised as a blind fiddler, with a bandage over his eyes, and he would attend him as his man to lead him. Thus accoutred, they reached the scene of action, where the blind fiddler was received with joyful shouts. They had plenty of meat and drink, and plied the fiddler and his man with more than was agreeable to them. Never was a more joyful wedding seen. They sung, they danced, told their stories, cracked jokes, &c., in a vein of humor more entertaining to the two guests than they probably could have found in any other meeting on a like occasion. When they were about to depart, they pulled out the leather pouches, and rewarded the fiddler very handsomely.

The next day the Dean and the Doctor walked out in their usual dress, and found their companions of the preceding evening scattered about in different parts of the road and the neighboring village, all begging their charity in doleful strains, and telling dismal stories of their distress. Among these they found some upon crutches, who had danced very nimbly at the wedding, others stone-blind, who were perfectly clear-sighted at the feast. The Doctor distributed among them the money which he had received as his pay; but the Dean, who mortally hated these sturdy vagrants, rated them soundly; told them in what manner he had been present at the wedding, and was let into their roguery; and assured them, if they did not immediately apply to honest labor, he would have them taken up and sent to gaol. Whereupon the lame once more recovered their legs, and the blind their eyes, so as to make a very precipitate retreat.

THE PIES.

Swift, in passing through the county of Cavan, called at a homely but hospitable house, where he knew he should be well received. The Lady Bountiful of the mansion, rejoiced to have so distinguished a guest, runs up to him, and with great eagerness and flippancy asks him what he will have for dinner. "Will you have an apple-pie, sir? Will you have a gooseberry-pie, sir? Will you have a cherry-pie, sir? Will you have a currant-pie, sir? Will you have a plum-pie, sir? Will you have a pigeon-pie, sir?" "Any pie, madam, but a *magpie*."

SHORT CHARITY SERMON.

The Dean once preached a charity sermon in St. Patrick's Cathedral, Dublin, the length of which disgusted many of his auditors; which, coming to his knowledge, and it falling to his lot soon after to preach another sermon of the like kind in the same place, he took special care to avoid falling into the former error. His text was, "He that hath pity upon the poor lendeth unto the Lord, and that which he hath given will he pay him again." The Dean, after repeating his text in a more than commonly emphatical tone, added, "Now, my beloved brethren, you hear the terms of this loan; if you like the security, down with your dust." The quaintness and brevity of the sermon produced a very large contribution.

A COURTIER'S RETORT.

While the prosecution for the Draper's fourth letter was depending, Swift one day waited at the Castle for an audience of Lord Carteret, the Lord Lieutenant, till his patience was exhausted; upon which he wrote the following couplet on a window, and went away:—

"My very good Lord, 'tis a very hard task,
For a man to wait here who has nothing to ask."

The Earl, upon this being shown to him, immediately wrote the following answer underneath:—

"My very good Dean, there are few who come here,
But have something to ask, or something to fear."

LYING.

Swift could not bear to have any lies told him, which his natural shrewdness and knowledge of the world generally enabled him to detect; and when the party attempted to palliate them, his usual reply was—"Come, come, don't attempt to darn your cobwebs."

DR. SACHEVERELL.

Some time after the expiration of Dr. Sacheverell's punishment, having been silenced three years from preaching, and his sermon ordered to be burned, the ministry treated him with great indifference, and he applied in vain for the vacant rectory of St. Andrew's, Holborn. Having, however, a slender acquaintance with Swift, he wrote to him for his interest with government in his behalf, stating how much he had suffered in the cause of the ministry. Swift immediately carried his letter to Lord Bolingbroke, then Secretary of State, who railed much at Sacheverell, calling him a busy intermeddling fellow; a prig and an incendiary, who had set the kingdom in a flame which could not be extinguished, and therefore deserved censure instead of reward. Although Swift had not a much better opinion of the Doctor than Lord Bolingbroke, he replied, "True, my Lord; but let me tell you a story. In a sea fight in the reign of Charles the Second, there was a very bloody engagement between the English and Dutch fleets, in the heat of which a Scotch sea-man was very severely bit by a louse on his neck, which he caught; and stooping down to crack it between his nails, many of the sailors near him had their heads taken off by a chain-shot from the enemy, which dashed their blood and brains about him; on which he had compassion upon the poor louse, returned him to his place and bid him live there at discretion, for as he had saved his life, he was bound in gratitude to save his." This recital threw my Lord Bolingbroke into a violent fit of laughing, who, when it was over, said, "The louse shall have the living for your story." And soon after Sacheverell was presented to it.

TAXING THE AIR.

Lady Carteret, wife of the Lord Lieutenant, said to Swift, "The air of Ireland is very excellent and healthy." "For God's sake, madam," said Swift, "don't say so in England; for if you do, they will certainly tax it."

WISDOM.

Wisdom (said the Dean) is a *fox*, who, after long hunting, will at last cost you the pains to dig out: it is a *cheese*, which, by how much the richer, has the thicker, the homelier, and the coarser coat, and whereof to a judicious palate the maggots are the best; it is a *sack-posset*, wherein the deeper you go you will find it the sweeter. Wisdom is a *hen*, whose cackling we must value and consider, because it is attended with an egg; but then, lastly, it is a *nut*, which, unless you choose with judgment, may cost you a tooth, and pay you with nothing but a worm.

EPITAPH ON JUDGE BOAT.

Here lies Judge *Boat* within a coffin,
Pray, gentlefolks, forbear your scoffin';
A *Boat* a judge! yes, where's the blunder
A *wooden* Judge is no such wonder!
And in his robes you must agree,
No *Boat* was better *dekt* than he.
'Tis needless to describe him fuller,
In short he was an able *sculler*.

ON STEPHEN DUCK, THE THRESHER AND FAVORITE POET.

The thresher Duck could o'er the Queen prevail,
The proverb says, "*no fence against a flail.*"
From *threshing* corn he turns to *thresh his brains*,
For which her Majesty allows him gains.
Though 'tis confest, that those who ever saw
His poems, think them all not worth a STRAW!

Thrice happy Duck, employed in threshing *stubble*,
Thy toil is lessen'd and thy profits double.

DIALOGUE BETWEEN SWIFT AND HIS LANDLORD.

The three towns of Navan, Kells, and Trim, which lay in Swift's route on his first journey to Laracor, seem to have deeply arrested his attention, for he has been frequently heard to speak of the beautiful situation of the first, the antiquity of the second, and the time-shaken towers of the third. There were three inns in Navan, each of which claims to this day the honor of having entertained Dr. Swift. It is probable that he dined at one of them, for it is certain that he slept at Kells, in the house of Jonathan Belcher, a Leicestershire man, who had built the inn in that town on the English model, which still exists, and, in point of capaciousness and convenience, would not disgrace the first road in England. The host, whether struck by the commanding sternness of Swift's appearance, or from natural civility, showed him into the best room, and waited himself at table. The attention of Belcher seems to have won so far upon Swift as to have produced some conversation. "You're an Englishman, Sir?" said Swift. "Yes, Sir." "What is your name?" "Jonathan Belcher, Sir." "An Englishman and Jonathan too, in the town of Kells —who would have thought it! What brought you to this country?" "I came with Sir Thomas Taylor, Sir; and I believe I could reckon fifty Jonathans in my family, Sir." "Then you are a man of family?" "Yes, Sir; I have four sons and three daughters by one mother, a good woman of true Irish mould." "Have you been long out of your native country?" "Thirty years, Sir." "Do you ever expect to visit it again?" "Never." "Can you say that without a sigh?" "I can, Sir; my family is my country!" "Why, Sir, you are a better philosopher than those who have written volumes on the subject. Then you are reconciled to your fate?" "I ought to be so; I am very happy; I like the people, and, though I was not born in Ireland, I'll die in it and that's the same thing." Swift paused in deep thought for near a minute, and then with much energy repeated the first line of the preamble of the noted Irish statute—*Ipsis Hibernis Hiberniores!*—("*The English*) *are more Irish than the Irish themselves.*"

ROGER COX.

What perhaps contributed more than any thing to Swift's enjoyment, was the constant fund of amusement he found in the facetious humor and oddity of the parish clerk, Roger Cox. Roger was originally a hatter in the town of Cavan, but, being of a lively jovial temper, and fonder of setting the fire-side of a village alehouse in a roar, over a tankard of ale or a bowl of whiskey, with his flashes of merriment and jibes of humor, than pursuing the dull routine of business to which fate had fixed him, wisely forsook it for the honorable function of a parish clerk, which he considered as an office appertaining in some wise to ecclesiastical dignity; since by wearing a band, no small part of the ornament of the Protestant clergy, he thought he might not unworthily be deemed, as it were, "*a shred of the linen vestment of Aaron.*" Nor was Roger one of those worthy parish clerks who could be accused of merely humming the psalms through the nostrils as a sack-butt, but much oftener instructed and amused his fellow-parishioners with the amorous ditties of the *Waiting Maid's Lamentation*, or one of those national songs which awake the remembrance of glorious deeds, and make each man burn with the enthusiasm of the conquering hero. With this jocund companion Swift relieved the tediousness of his lonesome retirement; nor did the easy freedom which he indulged with Roger ever lead his humble friend beyond the bounds of decorum and respect.

Roger's dress was not the least extraordinary feature of his appearance. He constantly wore a full-trimmed scarlet waistcoat of most uncommon dimensions, a light grey coat, which altogether gave him an air of singularity and whim as remarkable as his character.

To repeat all the anecdotes and witticisms which are recorded of the prolific genius of Roger in the simple annals of Laracor, would fill a little volume. He died at the good old age of ninety.

Soon after Swift's arrival at Laracor, he gave public notice that he would read prayers every Wednesday and Friday. On the first of those days after he had summoned his congregation, he ascended the desk, and after sitting some time with no other auditor than his clerk Roger, he rose up and with a composure and gravity that, upon this occasion, were irresistibly ridiculous, began—"Dearly beloved Roger, the Scripture moveth you and me in sundry places," and so proceeded to the end of the service. The story is not quite complete. But the fact is, that when he went into the church he found Roger *alone*, and exclaimed with evident surprise, "*What, Roger! none here but you?*" "*Yes, sir,*" replied Roger drily (turning over the book to find the lessons, for the day), "*sure you are here too.*"

ROGER AND THE POULTRY.

There happened, while Swift was at Laracor, the sale of a farm and stock, the farmer being dead. Swift chanced to walk past during the auction just as a pen of poultry had been put up. Roger bid for them, and was overbid by a farmer of the name of Hatch. "What, Roger, won't you buy the poultry?" exclaimed Swift. "No, sir," said Roger, "I see they are *just a'going to Hatch.*"

KELLY THE BLACKSMITH.

Although Roger took the lead, he did not monopolize all the wit, of the parish. It happened that Swift, having been dining at some little distance from Laracor, was returning home on horseback in the evening, which was pretty dark. Just before he reached Kellistown, a neighboring village, his horse lost a shoe. Unwillling to run the risk of laming the animal by continuing his ride in that condition, he stopped at one Kelly's, the blacksmith of the village, where, having called the man, he asked him if he could shoe a horse with a *candle.* "No," replied the smutty son of Vulcan, "but I can with a *hammer.*" Swift, struck with the reply, determined to have a little more conversation with him. Accordingly, he alighted and went into the cabin, which was literally rotten, but supported, wherever it had given way at different times, with pieces of timber. Swift, as was usual with him, began to rate poor Kelly soundly for his indolence in not getting his house put into better repair, in which the wife joined. "Hold, Doctor, for one moment!" exclaimed Kelly, "and tell me, whether you ever saw a *rotten* house *better* supported in all your life."

BIRTH-DAY PRESENTS.

It was for many years a regular custom with Swift's most intimate friends to make him some presents on his birth day. On that occasion, 30th November, 1732, Lord Orrery presented him with a paper book, finely bound, and Dr Delany with a silver standish, accompanied with the following verses;—

TO DR. SWIFT, WITH A PAPER BOOK, BY JOHN, EARL OF ORRERY

To thee, Dear Swift, those spotless leaves I send;
Small is the present, but sincere the friend.
Think not so poor a book below thy care;
Who knows the price that thou canst make it bear?
Tho' tawdry now, and like Tyralla's face,
The spacious front shines out with borrow'd grace;
Tho' pasteboards, glitt'ring like a tinsell'd coat,
A *rasa tabula* within denote;
Yet if a venal and corrupted age,
And modern vices should provoke thy rage;
If, warn'd once more by their impending fate,
A sinking country and an injured state
Thy great assistance should again demand,
And call forth Reason to defend the land;
Then shall we view these sheets with glad surprise
Inspired with thought, and speaking to our eyes:
Each vacant space shall then, enrichd, dispense
True force of eloquence and nervous sense;
Inform the judgment, animate the heart,
And sacred rules of policy impart.
The spangled cov'ring, bright with splendid ore,
Shall cheat the sight with empty show no more;
But lead us inward to those golden mines,
Where all thy soul in native lustre shines.

So when the eye surveys some lovely fair,
With bloom of beauty, graced with shape and air,
How is the rapture heighten'd when we find
The form excelled by her celestial mind!

VERSES LEFT WITH A SILVER STANDISH ON THE DEAN'S DESK, BY DR. DELANY.

Hither from Mexico I came,
To serve a proud Iernian dame;
Was long submitted to her will,
At length she lost me at Quadrille.
Through various shapes I often passed,
Still hoping to have rest at last;
And still ambitious to obtain
Admittance to the patriot Dean;
And sometimes got within his door,
But soon turn'd out to serve the poor;
Not strolling idleness to aid,
But honest industry decay'd.
At length an artist purchased me,
And wrought me to the shape you see.
  This done, to Hermes I applied:
"O Hermes! gratify my pride!
Be it my fate to serve a sage,
The greatest genius of his age;
That matchless pen let me supply,
Whose living lines will never die!"
  "I grant your suit," the god replied,
And here he left me to reside.

VERSES BY SWIFT, ON THE OCCASION.

A paper Book is sent by *Boyle*,
Too neatly gilt for me to soil:
Delany sends a Silver Standish,
When I no more a pen can brandish.

Let both around my tomb be placed,
As trophies of a muse deceas'd:
And let the friendly lines they writ,
In praise of long departed wit,
Be graved on either side in columns,
More to my praise than all my volumes;
To burst with envy, spite, and rage,
The Vandals of the present age.

THE DEAN'S CONTRIBUTORY DINNER.

Dean Swift once invited to dinner several of the first noblemen and gentlemen in Dublin. A servant announced the dinner, and the Dean led the way to the dining-room. To each chair was a servant, a bottle of wine, a roll, and an inverted plate. On taking his seat, the Dean desired the guests to arrange themselves according to their own ideas of precedence, and fall to. The company were astonished to find the table without a dish or any provisions. The Lord Chancellor, who was present, said, "Mr. Dean, we do not see the joke." "Then I will show it you," answered the Dean, turning up his plate, under which was half-a-crown and a bill of fare from a neighboring tavern. "Here, sir," said he, to his servant, "bring me a plate of goose." The company caught the idea, and each man sent his plate and half-a-crown. Covers, with everything that the appetites of the moment dictated, soon appeared. The novelty, the peculiarity of the manner, and the unexpected circumstances, altogether excited the plaudits of the noble guests, who declared themselves particularly gratified by the Dean's entertainment. "Well," said the Dean, "gentlemen, if you have dined, I will order *dessert.*" A large roll of paper, presenting the particulars of a splendid dinner, was produced, with an estimate of expense. The Dean requested the accountant-general to deduct the half-crowns from the amount, observing, "that as his noble guests were pleased to express their satisfaction with the dinner, he begged their advice and assistance in disposing of the *fragments* and *crumbs,*" as he termed the balance mentioned by the accountant-general—which was two hundred and fifty pounds. The company said, that no person was capable of instructing the Dean in things of that nature. After the circulation of the finest wines, the most judicious remarks on charity and its abuse were introduced, and it was agreed that the proper objects of liberal relief were well-educated families, who from affluence, or the expectation of it, were reduced through misfortune to silent despair. The Dean then divided the sum by the number of his guests, and addressed them according to their respective private characters, with which no one was, perhaps, better acquainted. "You, my Lords," said the Dean to several young noblemen, "I wish to introduce to some new acquaintance, who will at least make their acknowledgment for your favors with sincerity. You, my reverend Lords," addressing the bishops present, "adhere so closely to the spirit of the Scriptures, that your left hands are literally ignorant of the beneficence of your right. You, my Lord of Kildare, and the two noble lords near you, I will not entrust with any part of this money, as you have been long in the *usurious* habits of lending your own on such occasions; but your assistance, my Lord of Kerry, I must entrèat, as charity covereth a multitude of sins."

SWIFT AND BETTESWORTH.

Dean Swift having taken a strong dislike to Sergeant Bettesworth, revenged himself by the following lines in one of his poems:

> So at the bar the booby Bettesworth,
> Tho' half-a-crown o'erpays his sweat's worth,
> Who knows in law nor text nor margent,
> Calls Singleton his brother sergeant.

The poem was sent to Bettesworth, when he was in company with some of his friends. He read it aloud, till he had finished the lines relating to himself. He then flung it down with great violence, trembled and turned pale. After some pause, his rage for a while depriving him of utterance, he took out his penknife, and swore he would cut off the Dean's ears with it. Soon after he went to seek the Dean at his house; and not finding him at home, followed him to a friend's, where he had an interview with him. Upon entering the room, Swift desired to know his commands. "Sir," says he, "I am Sergeant Bet-tes-worth;" in his usual pompous way of pronouncing his name in three distinct syllables. "Of what regiment, pray?" says Swift. "O, Mr. Dean, we know your powers of raillery; you know me well enough, that I am one of his majesty's sergeants-at-law." "What then, sir?" "Why then, sir, I am come to demand of you, whether you are the author of this poem (producing it), and the villanous lines on me?" at the same time reading them aloud with great vehemence of emphasis, and much gesticulation. "Sir," said Swift, "it was a piece of advice given me in my early days by Lord Somers, never to own or disown any writing laid to my charge; because, if I did this in some cases, whatever I did not disown afterwards would infallibly be imputed to me as mine. Now, sir, I take this to have been a very wise maxim, and as such have followed it ever since; and I believe it will hardly be in the power of all your rhetoric, as great a master as you are of it, to make me swerve from that rule." Bettesworth replied, "Well, since you will give me no satisfaction in this affair, let me tell you, that your gown is alone your protection," and then left the room.

The sergeant continuing to utter violent threats against the Dean, there was an association formed and signed by all the principal inhabitants of the neighborhood, to stand by and support their generous benefactor against any one who should attempt to offer the least injury to his person or fortune. Besides, the public indignation became so strong against the sergeant, that although he had made a considerable figure at the bar, he now lost his business, and was seldom employed in any suit afterwards.

SWIFT AMONG THE LAWYERS.

Dean Swift having preached an assize sermon in Ireland, was invited to dine with the Judges; and having in his sermon considered the use and abuse of the law, he then pressed a little hard upon those counsellors, who plead causes which they knew in their consciences to be wrong. When dinner was over, and the glass began to go round, a young barrister retorted upon the dean; and after several altercations, the counsellor asked him, "If the devil was to die, whether a *parson* might not be found, who, for money, would preach his funeral?" "Yes," said Swift, "I would gladly be the man, and I would then give the *devil* his due, as I have this day done his *children*."

PREACHING PATRIOTISM.

Dean Swift is said to have jocularly remarked, that he never preached but twice in his life, and then they were not sermons, but pamphlets. Being asked, upon what subject? he replied, they were against Wood's halfpence. One of these sermons has been preserved, and is from this text, "As we have the opportunity, let us do good to all men." Its object was to show the great want of public spirit in Ireland, and to enforce the necessity of practising that virtue. "I confess," said he, "it was chiefly the consideration of the great danger we are in, which engaged me to discourse to you on this subject, to exhort you to a love of your country, and a public spirit, when all you have is at stake; to prefer the interest of your prince and your fellow subjects before that of one destructive impostor, and a few of his adherents.

"Perhaps it may be thought by some, that this way of discoursing is not so proper from the pulpit; but surely when an open attempt is made, and far carried on, to make a great kingdom one large poor-house; to deprive us of all means to excite hospitality or charity; to turn our cities and churches into ruins; to make this country a desert for wild beasts and robbers; to destroy all arts and sciences, all trades and manufactures, and the very tillage of the ground, only to enrich one obscure ill-designing projector, and his followers; it is time for the pastor to cry out that the wolf is getting into his flock, to warn them to stand together, and all to consult the common safety. And God be praised for his infinite goodness, in raising such a spirit of union among us at least in this point, in the midst of all our former divisions; which union, if it continues, will in all probability defeat the pernicious design of this pestilent enemy to the nation."

It will scarcely be credited, that this dreadful description, when stripped of its exaggerations, meant no more than that Ireland might lose about six thousand a year during Wood's patent for coining halfpence!

SWIFT AND HIS BUTLER

During the publication of the Drapers Letters, Swift was particularly careful to conceal himself from being known as the author. The only persons in the secret, were Robert Blakely, his butler, whom he employed as an amanuensis, and Dr. Sheridan. It happened, that on the very evening before the proclamation, offering a reward of £300 for discovering the author of these letters, was issued, Robert Blakely stopped out later than usual without his master's leave. The dean ordered the door to be locked at the accustomed hour, and shut him out. The next morning the poor fellow appeared before his master with marks of great contrition. Swift would hear no excuses, but abusing him severely, bade him strip off his livery, and quit the house instantly. "What!" said he, "is it because I am in your power that you dare to take these liberties with me? get out of my house, and receive the reward of your treachery."

Mrs. Johnson (Stella), who was at the deanery, did not interfere, but immediately dispatched a messenger to Dr. Sheridan, who on his arrival found Robert walking up and down the hall in great agitation. The doctor bade him not be uneasy, as he would try to pacify the dean, so that he should continue in his place. "That is not what vexes me," replied Robert, "though to be sure I should be sorry to lose so good a master; but what grieves me to the soul, is, that my master should have so bad an opinion of me, as to suppose me capable of betraying him for any reward whatever." When this was related to the dean, he was so struck with the honor and generosity of sentiment, which it exhibited in one so humble in life, that he immediately restored him to his situation, and was not long in rewarding his fidelity.

The place of verger to the cathedral becoming vacant, Swift called Robert to him, and asked him if he had any clothes of his own that were not a livery? Robert replying in the affirmative, he desired him to take off his livery, and put them on. The poor fellow, quite astonished, begged to know what crime he had committed, that he was to be discharged. The dean bade him do as he was ordered; and when he returned in his new dress, the dean called all the other servants into the room, and told them that they were no longer to consider him as their fellow-servant Robert, but as Mr. Blakely, verger of St. Patrick's Cathedral; an office which he had bestowed on him for his faithful services, and as a proof of that sure reward, which honesty and fidelity would always obtain.

HIS SATURNALIA.

Dean Swift, among other eccentricities, determined upon having a feast once a year, in imitation of the Saturnalia in ancient Rome. In this project he engaged several persons of rank, and his plan was put in execution at the deanery house. When all the servants were seated, and every gentleman placed behind his own servant, the Dean's footman, who presided, found fault with some meat that was not done to his taste; and imitating his master on such occasions, threw it at him. But the Dean was either so mortified by the reproof, or so provoked at the insult, that he flew into a violent passion, beat the fellow, and dispersed the whole assembly.—Thus abruptly terminated the Dean's Saturnalia.

THE DEAN AND FAULKNER.

George Faulkner, the Dublin printer, once called on Dean Swift on his return from London, dressed in a rich coat of silk brocade and gold lace, and seeming not a little proud of the adorning of his person: the Dean determined to humble him. When he entered the room, and saluted the Dean with all the respectful familiarity of an old acquaintance, the Dean affected not to know him; in vain did he declare himself as George Faulkner, the Dublin printer; the Dean declared him an impostor, and at last abruptly bade him begone. Faulkner, perceiving the error he had committed, intsantly returned home, and resuming his usual dress, again went to the Dean, when he was very cordially received. "Ah, George," said he, "I am so glad to see you, for here has been an impudent coxcomb, bedizened in silks and gold lace, who wanted to pass himself off for you; but I soon sent the fellow about his business; for I knew you to be *always* a plain dressed and honest man, just as you now appear before me."

SWIFT, ARBUTHNOT, AND PARNELL.

Swift, Arbuthnot, and Parnell, taking the advantage of a fine frosty morning, set out together upon a walk to a little place which Lord Bathurst had, about eleven miles from London. Swift, remarkable for being an old traveller, and for getting possession of the best rooms and warmest beds, pretended, when they were about half way, that he did not like the slowness of their pace; adding, that he would walk on before them, and acquaint his lordship with their journey. To this proposal they readily agreed; but as soon as he was out of sight, sent off a horseman by a private way (suspecting their friend's errand), to inform his lordship of their apprehensions. The man arrived in time enough to deliver his message before Swift made his appearance. His lordship then recollecting that the dean never had the smallpox, thought of the following stratagem. Seeing him coming up the avenue, he ran out to meet him, and expressed his happiness at the sight of him. "But I am mortified at one circumstance," continued his lordship, "as it must deprive me of the pleasure of your company; there is a raging small-pox in the house: I beg, however, that you will accept of such accommodation as a small house at the bottom of the avenue can afford you." Swift was forced to comply with this request: and in this solitary situation, fearful of speaking to any person around him, he was served with dinner. In the evening, the wits thought proper to release him, by going down to him in a body, to inform him of the deception, and to tell him that the first best room and bed in the house were at his service. Swift, though he might be inwardly chagrined, deemed it prudent to join in the laugh against himself; they adjourned to the mansion-house, and spent the evening in a manner easily to be conceived by those who are in the least acquainted with the brilliancy of their powers.

DEAN SWIFT AND THE PREACHER WHO STOLE HIS SERMON.

The eccentric Dean Swift, in the course of one of those journies to Holyhead, which, it is well known, he several times performed *on foot,* was travelling through Church Stretton, Shropshire, when he put up at the sign of the Crown, and finding the host to be a communicative good-humored man, inquired if there was any agreeable person in town, with whom he might partake of a dinner (as he had desired him to provide one), and that such a person should have nothing to pay. The landlord immediately replied, that the curate, Mr. Jones, was a very agreeable, companionable man, and would not, he supposed, have any objection to spend a few hours with a gentleman of his appearance. The Dean directed him to wait on Mr. Jones, with his compliments, and say that a traveller would be glad to be favored with his company at the Crown, if it was agreeable. When Mr. Jones and the Dean had dined, and the glass began to circulate, the former made an apology for an occasional absence, saying that at three o'clock he was to read prayers and preach at the church. Upon this intimation, the Dean replied, that he also should attend prayers. Service being ended, and the two gentlemen having resumed their station at the Crown, the Dean began to compliment Mr. Jones on his delivery of a very appropriate sermon; and remarked, that it must have cost him (Mr. Jones) some time and attention to compose such a one.

Mr. Jones observed, that his duty was rather *laborious*, as he served another parish church at a distance; which, with the Sunday and weekly service at Church Stretton, straitened him much with respect to the time necessary for the composition of sermons; so that when the subjects pressed, he could only devote a few days and nights to that purpose.

"Well," says the Dean, "it is well for you to have such a talent; for my part, the very sermon you preached this afternoon, cost me some *months* in the composing." On this observation, Mr. Jones began to look very gloomy, and to recognize his companion. "However," rejoined the

Dean, "don't you be alarmed; you have so good a talent at delivery, that I hereby declare, you have done more honor to my sermon this day, than I *could* do myself; and by way of compromising the matter, you must accept of this half-guinea for the justice you have done in the delivery of it."

SWIFT'S QUEER TESTIMONIAL TO HIS SERVANT.

Dean Swift, standing one morning at the window of his study, observed a decent old woman offer a paper to one of his servants, which the fellow at first refused in an insolent and surly manner. The woman however pressed her suit with all the energy of distress, and in the end prevailed. The dean, whose very soul was compassion, saw, felt, and was determined to alleviate her misery. He waited most anxiously for the servant to bring the paper; but to his surprise and indignation, an hour elapsed, and the man did not present it. The dean again looked out. The day was cold and wet, and the wretched petitioner still retained her situation, with many an eloquent and anxious look at the house. The benevolent divine lost all patience, and was going to ring the bell, when he observed the servant cross the street, and return the paper with the utmost *sang froid* and indifference. The dean could bear no longer; he threw up the sash, and loudly demanded what the paper contained. "It is a petition, please your reverence," replied the woman. "Bring it up, rascal!" cried the enraged dean. The servant, surprised and petrified, obeyed. With Swift, to know distress was to pity it; to pity to relieve. The poor woman was instantly made happy, and the servant almost as instantly turned out of doors, with the following written testimonial of his conduct. "The bearer lived two years in my service, in which time he was frequently drunk and negligent of his duty; which, conceiving him to be honest, I excused; but at last detecting him in a flagrant instance of cruelty, I discharge him." Such were the consequences of this paper, that for seven years the fellow was an itinerant beggar; after which the dean forgave him; and in consequence of another paper equally singular, he was hired by Mr. Pope, with whom he lived till death removed him.

SWIFT AT THOMASTOWN.

Dean Swift had heard much of the hospitable festivities of Thomastown, the seat of Mr. Matthew (See Anecdotes of Conviviality), from his friend Dr. Sheridan, who had been often a welcome guest, both on account of his convivial qualities, and as being the preceptor of the nephew of Mr. Matthew. He, at length, became desirous of ascertaining with his own eyes, the truth of a report, which he could not forbear considering as greatly exaggerated. On receiving an intimation of this from Sheridan, Mr. Matthew wrote a polite letter to the Dean, requesting the honor of a visit, in company with the doctor, at his next school vacation. They accordingly set out on horseback, attended by a gentleman who was a near relation to Mr. Matthew.

They had scarcely reached the inn where they intended to pass the first night, and which, like most of the Irish inns at that time, afforded but miserable entertainment, when they were surprised by the arrival of a coach and six horses, sent to convey them the remainder of the journey to Thomastown; and at the same time, bringing a supply of the choicest viands, wines, and other liquors, for their refreshment. Swift was highly pleased with this uncommon mark of attention paid him; and the coach proved particularly acceptable, as he had been a good deal fatigued with his day's journey.

When they came in sight of the house, the Dean, astonished at its magnitude, cried out, "What, in the name of God, can be the use of such a vast building?" "Why, Mr. Dean," replied the fellow traveller before mentioned, "there are no less than forty apartments for guests in that house, and all of them probably occupied at this time, except what are reserved for us." Swift, in his usual manner, called out to the coachman, to stop, and drive him back to Dublin, for he could not think of mixing with such a crowd. "Well," said he, immediately afterwards, "there is no remedy, I must submit, but I have lost a fortnight of my life."

Mr. Mathew received him at the door with uncommon marks of respect; and then conducting him to his apartments, after some compliments, made his usual speech, acquainting him with the customs of the house, and retired, leaving him in possession of his castle. Soon after, the cook appeared with his bill of fare, to receive his directions about supper; and the butler at the same time, with a list of wines, and other liquors. "And is all this really so?" said Swift, "and may I command here, as in my own house?" His companion assured him he might, and that nothing could be more agreeable to the owner of the mansion, than that all under his roof should live comformably to their own inclinations, without the least restraint. "Well then," said Swift, "I invite you and Dr. Sheridan to be my guests, while I stay; for I think I shall scarcely be tempted to mix with the mob below."

Three days were passed in riding over the demesne, and viewing the various improvements, without ever seeing Mr. Mathew, or any of the guests; nor were the company below much concerned at the dean's absence, as his very name usually inspired those who did not know him, with awe; and they were afraid that his presence would put an end to the ease and cheerfulness which reigned among them. On the fourth day, Swift entered the room where the company were assembled before dinner, and addressed Mr. Mathew, in a strain of the highest compliment, expatiating on all the beauties of his improvements, with all the skill of an artist, and with the taste of a connoisseur. Such an address for a man of Swift's character, could not fail of being pleasing to the owner, who was, at the same time, the planner of these improvements; and so fine an eulogium from one, who was supposed to deal more largely in satire, than panegyric, was likely to remove the prejudice entertained against his character, and prepossessed the rest of the company in his favor. He concluded his speech by saying: "And now, ladies and gentlemen, I am come to live among you, and it shall be no fault of mine, if we do not pass our time agreeably."

In a short time, all restraint on his account disappeared. He entered readily into all the little schemes for promoting mirth; and every day, with the assistance of his coadjutor, produced some new one, which afforded a good deal of sport and merriment. In short, never were such joyous scenes know at Thomastown before. When the time came, which obliged Sheridan to return to his school, the company were so delighted with the dean, that they earnestly entreated him to remain there some time longer; and Mr. Mathew himself for once broke through a rule which he observed, of never soliciting the stay of any guest. Swift found himself so happy, that he readily yielded to their solicitations; and instead of a fortnight, passed four months there, much to his satisfaction, and that of all those who visited the place during that time.

SWIFT'S LAST LINES.

In one of those lucid intervals which varied the course of Swift's unhappy lunacy, his guardians or physicians took him out to give him an airing. When they came to the Phœnix park, Swift remarked a new building which he had never seen, and asked what it was designed for? Dr. Kingsbury answered, "That, Mr. Dean, is the magazine for arms and powder, for the security of the city." "Oh! oh!" says the dean, pulling out his pocket-book, "let me take an item of that. This is worth remarking; my tablets, as Hamlet says, my tablets—memory, put down that." He then produced the following lines, being the last he ever wrote:

Behold! a proof of Irish sense!
Here Irish wit is seen,
When nothing's left for our defence,
We build a magazine.

The Dean then put up his pocket-book, laughing heartily at the conceit, and clenching it with, "After the steed's stolen, shut the stable door."

JOHN PHILPOT CURRAN.

HIS BIRTH

John Philpot Curran was born at Newmarket, a small village in the county of Cork, on the 24th of July, 1750. His father, James Curran, was seneschal of the manor, and possessed of a very moderate income. His mother was a very extraordinary woman. Eloquent and witty, she was the delight of her neighbors, and their chronicle and arbitress. Her stories were of the olden time, and made their way to the hearts of the people, who delighted in her wit and the truly national humor of her character. Little Curran used to hang with ecstasy upon his mother's accents, used to repeat her tales and her jests, and caught up her enthusiasm. After her death, he erected a monument over her remains, upon which the following memorial was inscribed:—

"Here lieth all that was mortal of Martha Curran—a woman of many virtues, few foibles, great talents, and no vice. This tablet was inscribed to her memory by a son who loved her, and whom she loved."

CURRAN AS PUNCH'S MAN.

Curran's first effort in public commenced when a boy in the droll character of Mr. Punch's man. It occurred in this way: One of the puppet-shows known as "Punch and Judy," arrived at Newmarket, to the great gratification of the neighborhood. Young Curran was an attentive listener at every exhibition of the show. At length, Mr. Punch's man fell ill, and immediately ruin threatened the establishment. Curran, who had devoured all the man's eloquence, offered himself to the manager as Mr. Punch's man. His services were gladly accepted, and his success so complete, that crowds attended every performance, and Mr. Punch's new man became the theme of universal panegyric.

CURRAN AT A DEBATING SOCIETY.

Curran's account of his introduction and *debut* at a debating society, is the identical "first appearance" of hundreds. "Upon the first of our assembling," he says, "I attended, my foolish heart throbbing with the anticipated honor of being styled 'the learned member that opened the debate,' or 'the very eloquent gentleman who has just sat down.' All day the coming scene had been flitting before my fancy, and cajoling it. My ear already caught the glorious melody of 'Hear him! hear him!' Already I was practising how to steal a sidelong glance at the tears of generous approbation bubbling in the eyes of my little auditory,—never suspecting, alas! that a modern eye may have so little affinity with moisture, that the finest gunpowder may be dried upon it. I stood up; my mind was stored with about a folio volume of matter; but I wanted a preface, and for want of a preface, the volume was never published. I stood up, trembling through every fibre: but remembering that in this I was but imitating Tully, I took courage, and had actually proceeded almost as far as 'Mr. Chairman,' when, to my astonishment and terror, I perceived that every eye was riveted upon me. There were only six or seven present, and the little room could not have contained as many more; yet was it, to my panic-stricken imagination, as if I were the central object in nature, and assembled millions were gazing upon me in breathless expectation. I became dismayed and dumb. My friends cried 'Hear him!' but there was nothing to hear. My lips, indeed, went through the pantomime of articulation; but I was like the unfortunate fiddler at the fair, who, coming to strike up the solo that was to ravish every ear, discovered that an enemy had maliciously soaped his bow; or rather, like poor Punch, as I once saw him, grimacing a soliloquy, of which his prompter had most indiscreetly neglected to administer the words." Such was the *debut* of "Stuttering Jack Curran," or "Orator Mum," as he was waggishly styled; but not many months elapsed ere the sun of his eloquence burst forth in dazzling splendor.

CURRAN AND THE BANKER-

A Limerick banker, remarkable for his sagacity, had an iron leg. "His leg," said Curran "is the *softest* part about him."

HIS DUEL WITH ST. LEGER.

Curran was employed at Cork to prosecute a British officer of the name of St. Leger, for an assault upon a Catholic clergyman. St. Leger was supected by Curran to be a creature of Lord Doneraile, and to have acted under the influence of his lordship's religious prejudice. Curran rated him soundly on this, and with such effect that St. Leger sent him a challenge the next day. They met, but as Curran did not return his fire, the affair ended. "It was not necessary," said Curran, "for me to fire at him, for he died in three weeks after the duel, of the *report of his own pistol.*"

THE MONKS OF THE SCREW.

This was the name of a club that met on every Saturday during term in a house in Kevin-street, and had for its members Curran, Grattan, Flood, Father O'Leary, Lord Charlemont, Judge Day, Judge Metge, Judge Chamberlaine, Lord Avonmore, Bowes Daly, George Ogle, and Mr. Keller. Curran, being Grand Prior of the order, composed the charter song as follows:—

When Saint Patrick our order created,
  And called us the Monks of the Screw,
Good rules he revealed to our Abbot,
  To guide us in what we should do.

But first he replenished his fountain
  With liquor the best in the sky:
And he swore by the word of his saintship
  That fountain should never run dry.

My children, be chaste till you're tempted—
  While sober, be wise and discreet—
And humble your bodies with fasting,
  Whene'er you've got nothing to eat.

Then be not a glass in the convent,
  Except on a festival, found—
And this rule to enforce, I ordain it
  A festival—*all the year round.*

LORD AVONMORE.

Curran was often annoyed when pleading before Lord Avonmore, owing to his lordship's habit of being influenced by first impressions. He and Curran were to dine together at the house of a friend, and the opportunity was seized by Curran to cure his lordship's habit of anticipating.

"Why, Mr. Curran, you have kept us a full hour waiting dinner for you," grumbled out Lord Avonmore. "Oh, my dear Lord, I regret it much; you must know it seldom happens, but—I've just been witness to a most melancholy occurrence." "My God! you seem terribly moved by it—take a glass of wine. What was it?—what was it?"—"I will tell you, my Lord, the moment I can collect myself. I had been detained at Court—in the Court of Chancery—your Lordship knows the Chancellor sits late." "I do, I do—but *go on*."—"Well, my Lord, I was hurrying here as fast as ever I could—I did not even change my dress—I hope I shall be excused for coming in my boots?" "Poh, poh—never mind your boots: the point—come at once to the point of the story."—"Oh—I will, my good Lord, in a moment. I walked here—I would not even wait to get the carriage ready—it would have taken time, you know. Now there is a market exactly in the road by which I had to pass—your Lordship may perhaps recollect the market—do you?" "To be sure I do—*go on*, Curran—*go on* with the story."—"I am very glad your Lordship remembers the market, for I totally forget the name of it—the name—the name—" "What the devil signifies the name of it, sir?—it's the Castle Market."—"Your Lordship is perfectly right—it is called the Castle Market. Well, I was passing through that very identical Castle Market, when I observed a butcher preparing to kill a calf. He had a huge knife in his hand—it was as sharp as a razor. The calf was standing beside him—he drew the knife to plunge it into the animal. Just as he was in the act of doing so, a little boy about four years old—his only son—the loveliest little baby I ever saw, ran suddenly across his path, and he killed—oh, my God! he killed—" "The child! the child! the child!" vociferated Lord Avonmore. "No, my Lord, *the calf*," continued Curran, very coolly; "he killed the calf, but—*your Lordship is in the habit of anticipating*."

HIS FIRST CLIENT.

When Curran was called to the bar, he was without friends, without connections, without fortune, conscious of talents far above the mob by which he was elbowed, and cursed with sensibility, which rendered him painfully alive to the mortifications he was fated to experience. Those who have risen to professional eminence, and recollect the impediments of such a commencement—the neglect abroad—the poverty, perhaps, at home—the frowns of rivalry—the fears of friendship—the sneer at the first essay—the prophecy that it will be the last—discouragement as to the present—forebodings as to the future—some who are established endeavoring to crush the chance of competition, and some who have failed anxious for the wretched consolation of companionship—those who recollect the comforts of such an apprenticeship may duly appreciate poor Curran's situation. After toiling for a very inadequate recompense at the Sessions of Cork, and wearing, as he said himself, his teeth almost to their stumps, he proceeded to the metropolis, taking for his wife and young children a miserable lodging on Hog-hill. Term after term, without either profit or professional reputation, he paced the hall of the Four Courts. Yet even thus he was not altogether undistinguished. If his pocket was not heavy, his heart was light—he was young and ardent, buoyed up not less by the consciousness of what he felt within, than by the encouraging comparison with those who were successful around him, and his station among the crowd of idlers, whom he amused with his wit or amused by his eloquence. Many even who had emerged from that crowd, did not disdain occasionally to glean from his conversation the rich and varied treasures which he did not fail to squander with the most unsparing prodigality; and some there were who observed the brightness of the infant luminary struggling through the obscurity that clouded its commencement. Among those who had the discrimination to appreciate, and the heart to feel for him, luckily for Curran, was Mr. Arthur Wolfe, afterwards the unfortunate, but respected Lord Kilwarden. The first fee of any consequence that he received was through his recommendation; and his recital of the incident cannot be without its interest to the young professional aspirant whom a temporary neglect may have sunk into dejection. "I then lived," said he, "upon Hog-hill; my wife and children were the chief furniture of my apartments; and as to my rent, it stood much the same chance of its liquidation with the national debt. Mrs. Curran, however, was a barrister's lady, and what was wanting in wealth, she was well determined should be supplied by dignity. The landlady, on the other hand, had no idea of any other gradation except that of pounds, shillings, and pence. I walked out one morning in order to avoid the perpetual altercations on the subject, with my mind, you may imagine, in no very enviable temperament. I fell into gloom, to which from my infancy I had been occasionally subject. I had a family for whom I had no dinner, and a landlady for whom I had no rent. I had gone abroad in despondence—I returned home almost in desperation. When I opened the door of my study, where *Lavater* alone could have found a library, the first object that presented itself was an immense folio of a brief, twenty golden guineas wrapped up beside it, and the name of *Old Bob Lyons* marked on the back of it. I paid my landlady—bought a good dinner—gave Bob Lyons a share of it; and that dinner was the date of my prosperity!"

CURRAN AND THE INFORMER.

The following is an extract from Curran's speech delivered before a committee of the house of Lords, against the Bill of attainder on Lord Edward's property:—

"I have been asked," said he, "by the committee, whether I have any defensive evidence? I am confounded by such a question. Where is there a possibility of obtaining defensive evidence? Where am I to seek it? I have often, of late, gone to the dungeon of the captive, but never have I gone to the grave of the dead, to receive instructions for his defence; nor, in truth, have I ever before been at the trial of a dead man! I offer, therefore, no evidence upon this inquiry, against the perilous example of which I do protest on behalf of the public, and against the cruelty and inhumanity and injustice of which I do protest in the name of the dead father, whose memory is sought to be dishonored, and of his infant orphans, whose bread is sought to be taken away. Some observations, and but a few, upon the evidence of the informer I will make. I do believe all he has admitted respecting himself. I do verily believe him in that instance, even though I heard him assert it upon his oath—by his own confession an informer, and a bribed informer—a man whom respectable witnesses had sworn in a court of justice, upon their oaths, not to be credible on his oath—a man upon whose single testimony no jury ever did, or ever ought to pronounce a verdict of guilty—a kind of man to whom the law resorts with abhorrence, and from necessity, in order to set the criminal against the crime, but who is made use of for the same reason that the most obnoxious poisons are resorted to in medicine. If such be the man, look for a moment at his story. He confines himself to mere conversation only, with a dead man! He ventures not to introduce any third person, living or even dead! he ventures to state no act whatever done. He wishes, indeed, to asperse the conduct of Lady Edward Fitzgerald; but he well knew that, even were she in this country, she could not be called as a witness to contradict him. See therefore, if there be any one assertion to which credit can be given, except this—that he has sworn and forsworn—that he is a traitor—that he has received five hundred guineas to be an informer, and that his general reputation is, to be utterly unworthy of credit."

He concludes thus:—"Every act of this sort ought to have a practical morality flowing from its principle. If loyalty and justice require that those children should be deprived of bread, must it not be a violation of that principle to give them food or shelter? Must not every loyal and just man wish to see them, in the words of the famous Golden Bull, 'always poor and necessitous, and for ever accompanied by the infamy of the father, languishing in continued indigence, and finding their punishment in living, and their relief in dying?' If the widowed mother should carry the orphan heir of her unfortunate husband to the gate of any man who himself touched with the sad vicissitude of human affairs, might feel a compassionate reverence for the noble blood that flowed in his veins, nobler than the royalty that first ennobled it, that, like a rich stream, rose till it ran and hid its fountain—if, remembering the many noble qualities of his unfortunate father, his heart melted over the calamities of the child—if his heart swelled, if his eyes overflowed, if his too precipitate hand was stretched forth by his pity or his gratitude to the excommunicated sufferers, how could he justify the rebel tear or the traitorous humanity? One word more and I have done. I once more earnestly and solemnly conjure you to reflect that the fact—I mean the fact of guilt or innocence which must be the foundation of this bill—is not now, after the death of the party, capable of being tried, consistent with the liberty of a free people, or the unalterable rules of eternal justice; and that as to the forfeiture and the ignominy which it enacts, that only can be punishment which lights upon guilt, and that can be only vengeance which breaks upon innocence."

Curran was one day setting his watch at the Post Office, which was then opposite the late Parliament House, when a noble member of the House of Lords said to him, "Curran, what do they mean to do with that useless building? For my part, I am sure I hate even the sight of it." "I do not wonder at it, my lord," replied Curran contemptuously; "I never yet heard of a *murderer* who was not afraid of a *ghost*."

LORD CLARE.

One day when it was known that Curran had to make an elaborate argument in Chancery, Lord Clare brought a large Newfoundland dog upon the bench with him, and during the progress of the argument he lent his ear much more to the dog than to the barrister. This was observed at length by the entire profession. In time the Chancellor lost all regard for decency; he turned himself quite aside in the most material part of the case, and began in full court to fondle the animal. Curran stopped at once. "Go on, go on, Mr. Curran," said Lord Clare. "Oh! I beg a thousand pardons, my Lord; I really took it for granted that your Lordship was *employed in consultation.*"

CURRAN'S ELOQUENCE.

In a debate on attachments in the Irish House of Commons, in 1785, Mr. Curran rose to speak against them; and perceiving Mr. Fitzgibon, the attorney-general (afterwards Lord Clare), had fallen asleep on his seat, he thus commenced:—"I hope I may say a few words on this great subject, without disturbing the sleep of any right honorable member; and yet, perhaps, I ought rather to envy than blame the tranquility of the right honorable gentleman. I do not feel myself so happily tempered, as to be lulled to repose by the storms that shake the land. If they invited any to rest, that rest ought not to be lavished on the guilty spirit."

Although Mr. Curran appears here to have commenced hostilities, it should be mentioned, that he was apprised of Mr. Fitzgibbon's having given out in the ministerial circles that he would take an opportunity during the debate, in which he knew that Mr. Curran would take a part, of *putting down the young patriot.* The Duchess of Rutland, and all the ladies of the castle were present in the gallery, to witness what Mr. Curran called, in the course of the debate, "this exhibition by command."

When Mr. Curran sat down, Mr. Fitzgibbon, provoked by the expressions he had used, and by the general tenor of his observation, replied with much personality, and among other things, denominated Mr. Curran a "*puny babbler.*" Mr. C. retorted by the following description of his opponent: "I am not a man whose respect in person and character depends upon the importance of his office; I am not a young man who thrusts himself into the fore-ground of a picture, which ought to be occupied by a better figure; I am not one who replies with invective, when sinking under the weight of argument; I am not a man who denies the necessity of parliamentary reform, at the time that he approves of its expediency, by reviling his own constituents, the parish clerk, the sexton, and the grave-digger; and if there be any man who can apply what I am not, to himself, I leave him to think of it in the committee, and contemplate upon it when he goes home."

The result of this night's debate was a duel between Mr. Curran and Mr. Fitzgibbon; after exchanging shots, they separated, but confirmed in their feeling of mutual aversion.

At the assizes at Cork, Curran had once just entered upon his case, and stated the facts to the jury. He then, with his usual impressiveness and pathos, appealed to their feelings, and was concluding the whole with this sentence: "Thus, gentlemen, I trust I have made the innocence of that persecuted man as clear to you as"—At that instant the sun, which had hitherto been over-clouded, shot its rays into the court-house—"as clear to you," continued he, "as yonder sun-beam, which now burst in among us, and supplies me with its splendid illustration."

SCENE BETWEEN FITZGIBBON AND CURRAN IN THE IRISH PARLIAMENT.

Mr. Fitzgibbon (afterwards Lord Clare) rose and said:—"The politically insane gentleman has asserted much, but he only emitted some effusions of the witticisms of fancy. His declamation, indeed, was better calculated for the stage of Sadler's Wells than the floor of the House of Commons. A mountebank, with but one-half of the honorable gentleman's talent for rant, would undoubtedly make his fortune. However, I am somewhat surprised he should entertain such a particular asperity against me, as I never did him a favor. But, perhaps, the honorable gentleman imagines he may talk himself into consequence; if so, I should be sorry to obstruct his promotion; he is heartily welcome to attack me. Of one thing only I will assure him, that I hold him in so small a degree of estimation, either as a man or as a lawyer, that I shall never hereafter deign to make him any answer."

Mr. Curran.—"The honorable gentleman says I have poured forth some witticisms of fancy. That is a charge I shall never be able to retort upon him. He says I am insane. For my part were I the man who, when all debate had subsided—who, when the bill was given up, had risen to make an inflammatory speech against my country, I should be obliged to any friend who would excuse my conduct by attributing it to insanity. Were I the man who could commit a murder on the reputation of my country, I should thank the friend who would excuse my conduct by attributing it to insanity. Were I a man possessed of so much arrogance as to set up my own little head against the opinions of the nation, I should thank the friend who would say, 'Heed him not, he is insane!' Nay, if I were such a man, I would thank the friend who had sent me to Bedlam. If I knew one man who was 'easily roused and easily appeased,' I would not give his character as that of the whole nation. The right honorable gentleman says he never came here with written speeches. I never suspected him of it, and I believe there is not a gentleman in the house, who, having heard what has fallen from him, would ever suspect him of writing speeches. But I will not pursue him further. I will not enter into a conflict in which victory can gain no honor."

HIS DEFENCE OF ARCHIBALD HAMILTON ROWAN.

The following extracts, commencing with a description of Mr. Rowan, will be found interesting:

"Gentlemen, let me suggest another observation or two, if still you have any doubt as to the guilt or the innocence of the defendant. Give me leave to suggest to you what circumstances you ought to consider, in order to found your verdict. You should consider the character of the person accused; and in this your task is easy. I will venture to say, there is not a man in this nation more known than the gentleman who is the subject of this persecution, not only by the part he has taken in public concerns, and which he has taken in common with many, but still more so by that extraordinary sympathy for human affliction which, I am sorry to think, he shares with so small a number. There is not a day that you hear the cries of your starving manufacturers in your streets, that you do not also see the advocate of their sufferings—that you do not see his honest and manly figure, with uncovered head soliciting for their relief: searching the frozen heart of charity for every string that can be touched by compassion, and urging the force of every argument and every motive, save that which his modesty suppresses—the authority of his own generous example. Or if you see him not there, you may trace his steps to the abode of disease, and famine, and despair; the messenger of Heaven—bearing with him food, and medicine, and consolation. Are these the materials of which we suppose anarchy and public rapine to be formed? Is this the man on whom to fasten the abominable charge of goading on a frantic populace to mutiny and bloodshed? Is this the man likely to apostatize from every principle that can bind him to the State—his birth, his property, his education, his character, and his children? Let me tell you, gentlemen of the jury, if you agree with his prosecutors in thinking there ought to be a sacrifice of such a man, on such an occasion, and upon the credit of such evidence you are to convict him, never did you, never can you, give a sentence consigning any man to public punishment with less danger to his person or to his fame; for where could the hireling be found to fling contumely or ingratitude at his head whose private distress he had not labored to alleviate, or whose public condition he had not labored to improve?"

Speaking of the liberty of the press, he says—

"What, then, remains? The liberty of the press only; that sacred Palladium, which no influence, no power, no government, which nothing but the folly or the depravity, or the folly or the corruption, of a jury ever can destroy. And what calamities are the people saved from by having public communication kept open to them! I will tell you, gentlemen, what they are saved from; I will tell you also to what both are exposed by shutting up that communication. In one case, sedition speaks aloud and walks abroad; the demagogue goes forth; the public eye is upon him; he frets his busy hour upon the stage; but soon either weariness, or bribe, or punishment, or disappointment, bears him down, or drives him off, and he appears no more. In the other case, how does the work of sedition go forward? Night after night the muffled rebel steals forth in the dark, and casts another brand upon the pile, to which, when the hour of fatal maturity shall arrive, he will apply the flame. If you doubt of the horrid consequences of suppressing the effusion of even iudividual discontent, look to those enslaved countries where the protection of despotism is supposed to be secured by such restraints. Even the person of the despot there is never in safety. Neither the fears of the despot, nor the machinations of the slave, have any slumber—the one anticipating the moment of peril, the other watching the opportunity of aggression. The fatal crisis is equally a surprise upon both; the decisive instant is precipitated without warning, by folly on the one side, or by frenzy on the other; and there is no notice of the treason till the traitor acts. In those unfortunate countries—one cannot read it without horror—there are officers whose province it is to have the water which is to be drunk by their rulers, sealed up in bottles, lest some wretched miscreant should throw poison into the draught. But, gentlemen, if you wish for a nearer and a more interesting example, you have it in the history of your own Revolution; you have it at that memorable period, when the monarch found a servile acquiescence in the ministers of his folly—when the liberty of the press was trodden under foot—when venal sheriffs returned packed juries to carry into effect those fatal conspiracies of the few against the many—when the devoted benches of public justice were filled by some of those foundlings of fortune, who, overwhelmed in the torrent of corruption at an early period, lay at the bottom like drowned bodies while sanity remained in them, but at length, becoming buoyant by putrefaction, they rose as they rotted, and floated to the surface of the polluted stream, where they were drifted along, the objects of terror and contagion and abomination.

"In that awful moment of a nation's travail, of the last gasp of tyranny, and the first breath of freedom, how pregnant is the example! The press extinguished, the people enslaved, and the prince undone! As the advocate of society therefore—of peace, of domestic liberty, and the lasting union of the two countries, I conjure you to guard the liberty of the press, that great sentinel of the State, that grand detector of public imposture: guard it, because when it sinks, there sink with it, in one common grave, the liberty of the subject and the security of the Crown.

"Gentlemen, I am glad that this question has not been brought forward earlier. I rejoice for the sake of the court, the jury, and of the public repose, that this question has not been brought forward till now. In Great Britain, analogous circumstances have taken place. At the commencement of that unfortunate war which has deluged Europe with blood, the spirit of the English people was tremblingly alive to the terror of French principles; at that moment of general paroxysm, to accuse was to convict. The danger loomed larger to the public eye from the misty region through which it was surveyed. We measure inaccessible heights by the shadows they project, when the lowness and the distance of the light form the length of the shade.

"There is a sort of aspiring and adventurous credulity, which disdains assenting to obvious truths, and delights in catching at the improbabilities of a case as its best ground of faith. To what other cause, gentlemen, can you ascribe that, in the wise, the reflecting, and the philosophic nation of Great Britain, a printer has been gravely found guilty of a libel for publishing those resolutions to which the present minister of that kingdom had already subscribed his name? To what other cause can you ascribe, what in my mind is still more astonishing, in such a country as Scotland—a nation, cast in the happy medium between the spiritless acquiescence of submissive poverty, and the sturdy credulity of pampered wealth—cool and ardent, adventurous and persevering, winging her eagle flight against the blaze of every science, with an eye that never winks, and a wing that never tires; crowned, as she is, with the spoils of every art and decked with the wreath of every muse, from the deep and scrutinizing researches of her Hume, to the sweet and simple, but not less sublime and pathetic, morality of her Burns—how, from the bosom of a country like that, genius and character and talents [Muir, Margarot, &c.,] should be banished to a distant and barbarous soil, condemned to pine under the horrid communion of vulgar vice, and base-born profligacy, twice the period that ordinary calculation gives to the continuance of human life! But I will not further press any idea that is painful to me, and I am sure must be painful to you; I will only say, you have now an example of which neither England nor Scotland had the advantage; you have the example of the panic, the infatuation, and the contrition of both. It is now for you to decide whether you will profit by their experience of idle panic and idle regret, or whether you meanly prefer to palliate a servile imitation of their frailty by a paltry affectation of their repentance. It is now for you to show that you are not carried away by the same hectic delusions, to acts of which no tears can wash away the fatal consequences or the indelible reproach."

He thus speaks of the Volunteers of Ireland:—

"Gentlemen, Mr. Attorney-General has thought proper to direct your attention to the state and circumstances of public affairs at the time of this transaction: let me also make a few retrospective observations on a period at which he has but slightly glanced You know, gentlemen, that France had espoused the cause of America, and we became thereby involved in a war with that nation.

'Heu, nescia mens hominum futuri!'

Little did that ill-fated monarch know that he was forming the first cause of those disastrous events that were to end in the subversion of his throne, in the slaughter of his family, and the deluging of his country with the blood of his people. You cannot but remember that a time when we had scarcely a regular soldier for our defence—when the old and young were alarmed and terrified with apprehensions of a descent upon our coasts—that Providence seemed to have worked a sort of miracle in our favor. You saw a band of armed men at the great call of nature, of honor, and their country; you saw men of the greatest wealth and rank; you saw every class of the community give up its members, and send them armed into the field to protect the public and private tranquility of Ireland; it is impossible for any man to turn back to that period, without reviving those sentiments of tenderness and gratitude which then beat in the public bosom; to recollect amidst what applause, what tears, what prayers, what benedictions, they walked forth amongst spectators, agitated by the mingled sensations of terror and of reliance, of danger and of protection, imploring the blessings of Heaven upon their heads, and its conquest upon their swords. That illustrious, and adored and abused body of men stood forward and assumed the title, which I trust the ingratitude of their country will never blot from its history—the Volunteers of Ireland."

He thus speaks of the national representation of the people;—

"Gentlemen, the representation of our people is the vital principle of their political existence; without it, they are dead, or they live only to servitude; without it, there are two estates acting upon and against the third, instead of acting in co-operation with it; without it, if the people are oppressed by their judges, where is the tribunal to which the offender shall be amenable?—without it, if they are trampled upon and plundered by a minister, where is the tribunal to which the offender shall be amenable?—without it, where is the ear to hear, or the heart to feel, or the hand to redress their sufferings? Shall they be found, let me ask you, in the accursed bands of imps and minions that bask in their disgrace, and fatten upon their spoils, and flourish upon their ruin? But let me not put this to you as a merely speculative question: it is a plain question of fact. Rely on it, physical man is everywhere the same: it is only the various operation of moral causes that gives variety to the social or individual character or condition. How otherwise happens it, that modern slavery looks quietly at the despot on the very spot where Leonidas expired? The answer is, Sparta has not changed her climate, but she has lost that goverment which her liberty could not survive."

Speaking of universal emancipation, he says:—

"This paper, gentlemen, insists on the necessity of emancipating the Catholics of Ireland; and that is charged as part of the libel. If they had waited another year—if they had kept this prosecution pending for another year, how much would remain for a jury to decide upon, I should be at a loss to discover. It seems as if the progress of public information was eating away the ground of prosecution. Since its commencement, this part of the libel has unluckily received the sanction of the Legislature. In that interval our Catholic brethren have re-obtained that admission which, it seems, it was a libel to propose. In what way to account for this I am really at a loss. Have any alarms been occasioned by the emancipation of our Catholic brethren? Has the bigoted malignity of any individual been crushed? Or has the stability of the goverment or that of the country been weakened? Or is one million of subjects stronger than four millions? Do you think that the benefit they have received, should be poisoned by the sting of vengeance. If you think so, you must say to them: You have demanded emancipation, and you have got it; but we abhor your persons; we are outraged at your success, and we will stigmatize by a criminal prosecution the adviser of that relief which you have obtained from the voice of your country. I ask you, do you think, as honest men anxious for the public tranquility, conscious that there are wounds not yet completely cicatrized, that you ought to speak this language at this time to men who are very much disposed to think that, in this very emancipation, they have been saved from their own Parliament by the humanity of their own sovereign? Or do you wish to prepare them for the revocation of these improvident concessions? Do you think it wise or humane at this moment to insult them, by sticking up in a pillory the man who dared to stand forth as their advocate? I put it to your oaths: Do you think that a blessing of that kind—that a victory obtained by justice over bigotry and oppression, should have a stigma cast upon it, by an ignominious sentence upon men bold enough and honest enough to propose that measure;—to propose the redeeming of religion from the abuses of the church, the reclaiming of three millions of men from bondage, and giving liberty to all who had a right to demand it; giving, I say, in the so much censured words of this paper—giving 'universal emancipation.'

"I speak in the spirit of the British law, which makes liberty commensurate with, and inseparable from, British soil—which proclaims even to the stranger and sojourner, the moment he sets his foot upon British earth, that the ground on which he treads is holy, and consecrated by the genius of universal emancipation. No matter in what language his doom may have been pronounced—no matter what complexion, incompatible with freedom, an Indian or an African sun may have burnt on him—no matter in what disastrous battle the helm of his liberty may been cloven down—no matter with what solemnities he may have been devoted upon the altar of slavery—the moment he touches the sacred soil of Britain, the altar and the god sink together in the dust; his soul walks abroad in its own majesty; his body swells beyond the measure of his chains, which burst from around him, and he stands redeemed, regenerated, and disenthralled by the irresistible genius of UNIVERSAL EMANCIPATION."

(Mr. Curran was here interrupted with the loud and irresistible acclamations of all within hearing. When, after a long interval, the enthusiasm had in some degree subsided, he thus modestly alluded to the incident).

"Gentlemen, I am not such a fool as to ascribe any effusion of this sort to any merit of mine. It is the mighty theme, and not the inconsiderable advocate, that can excite interest in the hearer: what you hear is but the testimony which nature bears to her own character; it is the effusion of her gratitude to that power which stamped that character upon her."

He concludes with this brilliant peroration:—

"Upon this subject, therefore, credit me when I say I am still more anxious for you than I can possibly be for him. Not the jury of his own choice, which the law of England allows, but which ours refuses, collected in that box by a person certainly no friend to Mr. Rowan—certainly not very deeply interested in giving him a very impartial jury. Feeling this, as I am persuaded you do, you cannot be surprised, however you may be distressed, at the mournful presage with which an anxious public is led to fear the worst from your possible determination. But I will not, for the justice and honor of our common country, suffer my mind to be borne away by such melancholy anticipation. I will not relinquish the confidence that this day will be the period of his sufferings; and, however mercilessly he has been hitherto pursued, that your verdict will send him home to the arms of his family and the wishes of his country. But if, which Heaven forbid! it hath still been unfortunately determined, that because he has not bent to power and authority, because he would not bow down before the golden calf and worship it, he is to be bound and cast into the furnace,—I do trust in God there is a redeeming spirit in the constitution, which will be seen to walk with the sufferer through the flames, and to preserve him unhurt by the conflagration."

After this brilliant speech, when Curran made his appearance outside the court, he was surrounded by the populace, who had assembled to chair him. He begged of them to desist, in a commanding tone; but a gigantic chairman, eyeing Curran from top to toe, cried out to his companion—

"Arrah, blood and turf! Pat, don't mind the little darlin'; pitch him upon *my* shoulder." He was, accordingly, carried to his carriage, and drawn home by the people.

ENCOUNTER WITH A FISHWOMAN.

There was a fishwoman in Cork who was more than a match for the whole fraternity of her order. She could only be matched by Mrs. Scutcheen, of Patrick-street, Dublin—the lady who used to boast of her "bag of farthin's," and regale herself before each encounter with a pennorth of the "droppin's o' the cock." Curran was passing the quay at Cork where this virago held forth, when, stopping to listen to her, he was requested to "go on ou' that." Hesitating to retreat as quick as the lady wished, she opened a broadside upon Curran, who returned fire with such effect as to bring forth the applause of the surrounding sisterhood. She was vanquished for the first time, though she had been "thirty years on the stones o' the quay."

CURRAN AND LORD ERSKINE.

Dr. Crolly, in speaking of the two great forensic orators of the day, drawns a comparison between the circumstances under which both addressed their audiences:—

"When Erskine pleaded, he stood in the midst of a secure nation, and pleaded like a priest of the temple of justice, with his hand on the altar of the constitution, and all England waiting to treasure every deluding oracle that came from his lips. Curran pleaded—not in a time when the public system was only so far disturbed as to give additional interest to his eloquence—but in a time when the system was threaetned with instant dissolution; when society seemed to be falling in fragments round him; when the soil was already throwing up flames. Rebellion was in arms. He pleaded, not on the floor of a shrine, but on a scaffold; with no companions but the wretched and culpable beings who were to be flung from it, hour by hour; and no hearers but the crowd, who rushed in desperate anxiety to that spot of hurried execution—and then rushed away, eager to shake off all remembrance of scenes which had torn every heart among them."

HIS DUEL WITH BULLY EGAN.

When Curran and Bully Egan met on the ground, the latter complained of the advantage his antagonist had over him, and declared that he was as easily hit as a turf stack, while, as to firing at Curran, he might as well fire at a razor's edge. Whereupon, Curran waggishly proposed that his size should be chalked out upon Egan's side, and that "every shot which hits outside that mark should *go for nothing!*"

MASSY VERSUS HEADFORT.

The following extract is from his celebrated speech against the Marquis of Headfort:—

"Never so clearly as in the present instance, have I observed that safeguard of justice which Providence has placed in the nature of man. Such is the imperious dominion with which truth and reason wave their sceptre over the human intellect, that no solicitation, however artful—no talent, however commanding—can seduce it from its allegiance. In proportion to the humility of our submission to its rule, do we rise into some faint emulation of that ineffable and presiding Divinity, whose characteristic attribute it is to be coerced and bound by the inexorable laws of its own nature, so as to be *all-wise* and *all-just* from necessity rather than election. You have seen it in the learned advocate who has preceded me, most peculiarly and strikingly illustrated. You have seen *even* his great talents, perhaps the first in any country, languishing under a cause too weak to *carry* him, and too heavy to be *carried* by him. He was forced to dismiss his natural candor and sincerity, and, having no merits in his case, to take refuge in the dignity of his own manner, the resources of his own ingenuity, from the overwhelming difficulties with which he was surrounded. Wretched client! unhappy advocate! what a combination do you form! But such is the condition of guilt—its commission mean and tremulous—its defence artificial and insincere—its prosecution candid and simple—its condemnation dignified and austere. Such has been the defendant's guilt—such his defence—such shall be my address to you—and such, I trust, your verdict. The learned counsel has told you that this unfortunate woman is not to be estimated at forty thousand pounds. Fatal and unquestionable is the truth of this assertion.

Alas! gentlemen, she is no longer worth anything; faded, fallen, degraded, and disgraced, she is worth less than nothing! But it is for the honor, the hope, the expectation, the tenderness, and the comforts that have been blasted by the defendant, and have fled forever, that you are to remunerate the plaintiff by the punishment of the defendant. It is not her present value which you are to weigh; but it is her value at that time when she sat basking in a husband's love, with the blessing of Heaven on her head, and its purity in her heart; when she sat amongst her family, and administered the morality of the parental board. Estimate that past value — compare it with its present deplorable diminution—and it may lead you to form some judgment of the severity of the injury, and the extent of the compensation.

"The learned counsel has told you, you ought to be cautious, because your verdict cannot be set aside for excess. The assertion is just; but has he treated you fairly by its application? His cause would not allow him to be fair; for why is the rule adopted in this single action? Because, this being peculiarly an injury to the most susceptible of all human feelings, it leaves the injury of the husband to be ascertained by the sensibility of the jury, and does not presume to measure the justice of their determination by the cold and chilly exercise of its own discretion. In any other action it is easy to calculate. If a tradesman's arm is cut off, you can measure the loss he has sustained; but the wound of feeling, and the agony of the heart, cannot be judged by any standard with which I am acquainted. And you are unfairly dealt with when you are called on to appreciate the present sufferings of the husband by the present guilt, delinquency, and degradation of his wife. As well might you, if called on to give compensation to a man for the murder of his dearest friend, find the measure of his injury by weighing the ashes of the dead. But it is not, gentlemen of the jury, by weighing the ashes of the dead that you would estimate the loss of the survivor.

"The learned counsel has referred you to other cases and other countries, for instances of moderate verdicts. I can refer you to some authentic instances of just ones. In the next county, £15,000 against a subaltern officer. In Travers and Macarthy, £5,000 against a servant. In

Tighe against Jones, £1,000 against a man not worth a shilling. What, then, ought to be the rule, where rank and power, and wealth and station, have combined to render the example of his crime more dangerous—to make his guilt more odious—to make the injury to the plaintiff more grievous, because more conspicuous? I affect no levelling familiarity, when I speak of persons in the higher ranks of society—distinctions of orders are necessary, and I always feel disposed to treat them with respect—but when it is my duty to speak of the crimes by which they are degraded, I am not so fastidious as to shrink from their contact, when to touch them is essential to their dissection. However, therefore, I should feel on any other occasion, a disposition to speak of the noble defendant with the respect due to his station, and perhaps to his qualities, of which he may have many to redeem him from the odium of this transaction, I cannot so indulge myself here. I cannot betray my client, to avoid the pain of doing my duty. I cannot forget that in this action the condition, the conduct, and circumstances of the parties, are justly and peculiarly the objects of your consideration. Who, then, are the parties?

The plaintiff, young, amiable, of family and education. Of the generous disinterestedness of his heart you can form an opinion even from the evidence of the defendant, that he declined an alliance which would have added to his fortune and consideration, and which he rejected for an unportioned union with his present wife—she too, at that time, young, beautiful and accomplished; and feeling her affection for her husband increase, in proportion as she remembered the ardor of his love, and the sincerity of his sacrifice. Look now to the defendant! Can you behold him without shame and indignation? With what feelings can you regard a rank that he has so tarnished, and a patent that he has so worse than cancelled? High in the army—high in the state—the hereditary counsellor of the King—of wealth incalculable—and to this last I advert with an indignant and contemptuous satisfaction, because, as the only instrument of his guilt and shame, it will be the means of his punishment, and the source of his compensation."

THE SERENADING LOVER.

In the very zenith of Curran's professional

career, he was consulted in a case of extremely novel character, which arose out of the following circumstances:—

Not many doors from Eden Quay, in Upper Sackville-street, lived a young lady of very fascinating manners, and whose beauty had attracted considerable attention wherever she made her appearance. Amongst the many gentlemen whose hearts she had touched, and whose heads she had deranged, was one young Englishman, a graduate of Trinity College, and about as fair a specimen of the reverse of beauty as ever took the chair at a dinner of the Ugly Fellows' Club. Strange to say, he above all others was the person on whom she looked with any favor. Men of rank and fortune had sought her hand—lords and commoners had sought the honor of an introduction; but no!—none for her but the ugly man! In vain did the ladies of her acquaintance quiz her about her taste—in vain did her family remonstrate upon the folly of her conduct, in refusing men of station for such an individual—no go! none for her but the ugly man! Her dear papa only seemed to take the affair in a quiet way; not that he was indifferent about the matter, but he loved her too much to throw any obstacle in the way of her happiness. Not so, however, with her brother—a splendid young fellow, whose mortification was intense, especially as the whole affair was the theme of ridicule among his fellow-students in Old Trinity. He, though sharing in all the love and tenderness of the father, could not understand his quiet resignation. Was is it to be thought of that one who was the butt of the University—one on whom nature had played her fantastic tricks, should be the person who held the key to his lovely sister's heart? No! the father might resign himself to his quiet philosophy, but *he*, at least, would have none of it. It should never be said within the college walls that he looked tamely on while a farce of this kind was being played out, especially as some of his most intimate fellow-students, and a beloved one in particular, took more than a common interest in the matter.

On a summer morning, in the middle of July, he was coming out of his hall-door, when the postman handed him two letters, one of which was directed to his sister. Suspecting the party from whom it came, and that a knowledge of its contents might lead to some discovery useful to him in frustrating the writer's designs, he opened it, and found that his suspicion was correct, and that himself was the object of complaint for his manner towards him in college; and further, that, as he was about to leave for England on the following day, and would not return for some weeks, he would do himself the honor of serenading her at twelve o'clock that night. After reading the letter, his first thought was to look to the condition of his horsewhip; but, after a little quiet reflection, he resolved upon another plan of action.

Breakfast over, he proceeded to the kitchen, summoned all the servants to his presence, to whom he related the whole story from beginning to end, and proposed that they should drench him with water when he made his appearance under the window. But there happened to be among them a corpulent lady called Betty Devine, who entered a plea of objection to that mode of proceeding on the ground of "waste of water;" that in *Edinburgh*, where she had served for seven years, they wouldn't think of such waste; and that, if the young master would only leave the matter in *her* hands, she would *drown* the musician in a chorus, the like of which was not to be heard outside the boundaries of bonnie Scotland. To this proposition on the part of Betty the young gentleman gave a hearty assent; adding, at the same time, a hope that her want of practice since she left *Edinburgh* would be no obstacle to her success. To which Miss Devine replied, by asking him to name the window out of which she was to present her *compliments* to the English minstrel. "As to that, Betty," said he, "I leave you to select your own ground; but take care that you dont miss fire"—an observation which took the stable-boy, Bill Mack, by the greatest surprise, as, from Betty's powers of administration in his regard, a *faded* dark-brown coat the master gave him had been restored to its original color.

For once in her life-time Betty found herself mistress of her situation, and having made her arrangements, despatched Bill Mack with an invitation to some of her sable friends of the Quay to witness the forthcoming concert at twelve o'clock that night.

Scarcely had the hour arrived, however, when the serenader made his appearance, dressed in the pink of fashion; and, placing himself under his lady's window, proceeded to play the guitar in the best style. The performance hadn't well commenced, when, throwing

> "his eye
> To her lattice high,"

he beheld a female figure at the two-pair window, which she opened gently. Then commenced his best efforts in the "art divine." No doubt it was the lady of his love that was there, about to reward him with

> "Nature's choice gifts from above,"

—not the wax artificials of these days, but the *real gems*, which he hoped to preserve on his passage to England!

That he saw a female figure was but too true: it was Miss Betty Devine, who had been arranging that portion of her toilet which might endanger the free exercise of her right arm. This done, Miss Devine stood forward, and, grasping a certain utensil of more than ordinary proportions, with one bound, not only "returned its *lining* on the night," as Tom Moore says, but also on the head of the devoted serenader, who was so stunned by Betty's favor, that it was some time before he realized the nature of the gift. His nasal organ having settled all doubt in that respect, he made his way from the crowd, vowing law and vengeance. "What is the matter?" asked a popular commoner, on his way from the parliament house, to one of the boys of the Quay; "It's a consart, yer honor, given by Betty de Scotch girl; de creature's fond o' harmony; and for my part, de tung is stickin' to de roof of my mout from de fair dint of de corus! I didn't taste a drop since mornin'. Ay boys, aint ye all dry?" This appeal having met with a favorable response, the gentlemen of the Quay retired to drink "his honor's health, and to wash down de music!"

Meanwhile, the next morning the serenading gentleman went in all haste to his brother-in-law, one of the leading merchants of the city, to whom he communicated the occurrence of the previous night. He had scarcely finished, when the merchant took him off to his attorney who, without further delay, went with them to the residence of Curran, to have his opinion on the case. When they had finished, Curran at once gave his opinion. "Gentlemen," said he, "in this country, when we go to see a friend or acquaintance, all we ever expect is—POT LUCK!"

Carew O'Dwyer was the first who had the honor of proposing that Curran's remains should be brought over from England and laid in Glasnevin.

Charles Phillips' first introduction to Curran took place at the Priory, a country villa about four miles from Dublin. Curran would have no one to introduce him, but went and took him by the hand.

Lundy Foot, the tobacconist, was on the table, under examination, and, hesitating to answer—"Lundy, Lundy," said Curran, "that's a poser—a devil of a pinch."

EMPLOYMENT OF INFORMERS.

"I speak not of the fate of those horrid wretches who have been so often transferred from the table to the dock, and from the dock to the pillory; I speak of what your own eyes have seen, day after day, during the course of this commission, from the box where you are now sitting; the number of horrid miscreants who avowed, upon their oaths, that they had come from the seat of government—from the Castle—where they had been worked upon by the fear of death and the hopes of compensation, to give evidence against their fellows; that the mild and wholesome councils of this government are holden over these catacombs of living death, where the wretch that is buried a man lies till his heart has time to fester and dissolve, and is then dug up a witness. Is this fancy, or is it fact? Have you not seen him after his resurrection from that tomb, after having been dug out of the region of death and corruption, make his appearance upon the table, the living image of life and of death, and the supreme arbiter of both? Have you not marked, when he entered, how the stormy wave of the multitude retired at his approach? Have you not marked how the human heart bowed to the supremacy of his power, in the undissembled homage of deferential horror? How his glance, like the lightning of heaven, seemed to rive the body of the accused, and mark it for the grave, while his voice warned the devoted wretch of life and death—a death which no innocence can escape, no art elude, no force resist, no antidote preserve? There was an antidote—a juror's oath; but even that adamantine chain, which bound the integrity of man to the throne of eternal justice, is solved and molten in the breath that issues from the informer's mouth; conscience swings from her mooring, and the appalled and affrighted juror consults his own safety in the surrender of his victim. * * Informers are worshipped in the temple of justice, even as the devil has been worshipped by pagans and savages—even so, in this wicked country, is the informer an object of judicial idolatry—even so is he soothed by the music of human groans—even so is he placated and incensed by the fumes and by the blood of human sacrifices."

CURRAN AND THE FARMER.

A farmer attending a fair with a hundred pounds in his pocket, took the precaution of depositing it in the hands of the landlord of the public-house at which he stopped. Next day he applied for the money, but the host affected to know nothing of the business. In this dilemma the farmer consulted Curran. "Have patience, my friend," said the counsel; "speak to the landlord civilly, and tell him you are convinced you must have left your money with some other person. Take a friend with you, and lodge with him another hundred, and then come to me." The dupe doubted the advice; but, moved by the authority or rhetoric of the learned counsel, he at length followed it. "And now, sir," said he to Curran, "I don't see as I am to be better off for this, if I get my second hundred again; but how is that to be done?" "Go and ask him for it when he is alone," said the counsel. "Ay, sir, but asking won't do, I'ze afraid, without my witness, at any rate." "Never mind, take my advice," said Curran; "do as I bid you, and return to me." The farmer did so, and came back with his hundred, glad at any rate to find that safe again in his possession. "Now, sir, I suppose I must be content; but I don't see as I am much better off." "Well, then," said the counsel, "now take your friend with you, and ask the landlord for the hundred pounds your friend saw you leave with him." It need not be added, that the wily landlord found that he had been taken off his guard, whilst the farmer returned exultingly to thank his counsel, with both hundreds in his pocket.

CURRAN AND THE JUDGE.

Soon after Mr. Curran had been called to the bar, on some statement of Judge Robinson's, the young counsel observed, that "he had never met the law, as laid down by his Lordship, in any book in his library." "That may be, sir," said the Judge; "but I suspect that your library is very small." Mr. Curran replied, "I find it more instructive, my Lord, to study good works than to compose bad ones.* My books may be few; but the title-pages give me the writers' names, and my shelf is not disgraced by any such rank absurdities, that their very authors are ashamed to own them." "Sir," said the Judge, "you are forgetting the respect which you owe to the dignity of the judicial character." "Dignity!" exclaimed Mr. Curran; "My Lord, upon that point I shall cite you a case from a book of some

* Judge Robinson was the author of many stupid, slavish, and scurrilous political pamphlets; and, by his demerits, raised to the eminence which he thus disgraced. —*Lord Brougham.*

anthority, with which you are, perhaps, not unacquainted." He then briefly recited the story of Strap, in *Roderick Random*, who having stripped off his coat to fight, entrusted it to a bystander. When the battle was over, and he was well beaten, he turned to resume it, but the man had carried it off. Mr. Curran thus applied the tale:—"So, my Lord, when the person entrusted with the dignity of the judgment-seat lays it aside for a moment to enter into a disgraceful personal contest, it is in vain when he has been worsted in the encounter that he seeks to resume it—it is in vain that he tries to shelter himself behind an authority which he has abandoned." "If you say another word, I'll commit you," replied the angry Judge; to which Mr. C. retorted, "If your Lordship shall do so, we shall both of us have the consolation of reflecting, that I am not the worst thing your Lordship has committed."

CURRAN'S QUARREL WITH FITZGIBBON.

Curran distinguished himself not more as a barrister than as a member of parliament; and in the latter character it was his misfortune to provoke the enmity of a man, whose thirst for revenge was only to be satiated by the utter ruin of his adversary. In the discussion of a bill of a penal nature, Curran inveighed in strong terms against the Attorney-General, Fitzgibbon, for *sleeping on the bench* when statutes of the most cruel kind were being enacted; and ironically lamented that the slumber of guilt should so nearly resemble the repose of innocence. A challenge from Fitzgibbon was the consequence of this sally; and the parties having met, were to fire when they chose. "I never," said Curran, when relating the circumstances of the duel,—"I never saw any one whose determination seemed more malignant than Fitzgibbon's. After I had fired, he took aim at me for at least half a minute; and on its proving ineffectual, I could not help exclaiming to him, 'It was not your fault, Mr Attorney; you were deliberate enough.'" The Attorney-General declared his honor satisfied; and here, at least for the time, the dispute appeared to terminate.

Not here, however, terminated Fitzgibbon's animosity. Soon afterwards, he became Lord

Chancellor, and a peer of Ireland, by the title of Lord Clare; and in the former capacity he found an opportunity, by means of his judicial authority, of ungenerously crushing the rising powers and fortunes of his late antagonist. Curran, who was at this time a leader, and one of the senior practitioners at the Chancery Bar, soon felt all the force of his rival's vengeance. The Chancellor is said to have yielded a reluctant attention to every motion he made; he frequently stopped him in the middle of a speech, questioned his knowledge of law, recommended to him more attention to facts, in short, succeeded not only in crippling all his professional efforts, but actually in leaving him without a client. Curran, indeed, appeared as usual in the three other courts [of the "Four Courts" at Dublin]; but he had been already stripped of his most profitable practice, and as his expenses nearly kept pace with his gains, he was almost left a beggar, for all hopes of the wealth and honors of the long-robe were now denied him. The memory of this persecution embittered the last moments of Curran's existence; and he could never even allude to it, without evincing a just and excusable indignation.

In a letter which he addressed to a friend, twenty years after, he says, "I made no compromise with power; I had the merit of provoking and despising the personal malice of every man in Ireland who was the known enemy of the country. Without the walls of the court of justice, my character was pursued with the most persevering slander; and within those walls, though I was too strong to be beaten down by any judicial malignity, it was not so with my clients, and my consequent losses in professional income have never been estimated at less, as you must have often heard, than £30,000."

HIGH AUTHORITY.

Curran was once engaged in a legal argument; behind him stood his colleague, a gentleman whose person was remarkably tall and slender, and who had originally intended to take holy orders. The Judge observing that the case under discussion involved a question of ecclesiastical law,—"Then," said Curran, "I can refer your Lordship to a high authority behind me, who was intended for the church, though in my opinion he was fitter for the steeple."

USE OF RED TAPE.

Curran, when Master of the Rolls, said to Mr. Grattan, "You would be the greatest man of your age, Grattan, if you would buy a few yards of red tape, and tie up your bills and papers."

CURRAN AND THE MASTIFF.

Curran used to relate with infinite humor an adventure between him and a mastiff, when he was a boy. He had heard somebody say that any person throwing the skirts of his coat over his head, stooping low, holding out his arms, and creeping along backwards, might frighten the fiercest dog, and put him to flight. He accordingly made the attempt on a miller's animal in the neighborhood, who *would never let the boys rob the orchard;* but found to his sorrow that he had a dog to deal with which did not care what end of a boy went foremost, so that he could get a good bite out of it. "I pursued the instructions," said Curran, "and as I had no eyes save those in front, fancied the mastiff was in full retreat; but I was confoundedly mistaken; for at the very moment I thought myself victorious, the enemy attacked my rear, and having got a reasonably good mouthful out of it, was fully prepared to take another before I was rescued. Egad, I thought for a time the beast had devoured my entire centre of gravity, and that I should never go on a steady perpendicular again." "Upon my word," said Sir Jonah Barrington, to whom Curran related this story, "the mastiff may have left you your centre, but he could not have left much gravity behind him, among the bystanders."

ARTHUR O'LEARY.

ARTHUR O'LEARY was born in the year 1729, at Acres in the parish of Fanlobbus, near Dunmanway, in the western part of the County of Cork. His parents were undistinguished amongst the industrious and oppressed peasantry, who at the time of his birth suffered under the operation of the penal laws. The family from which he descended was early distinguished in Irish history; but if his immediate ancestors ever enjoyed a higher rank in the social scale than that which is derived from successful industry, their circumstances had changed long before his birth, as a name which excited the respect of his countrymen, and a mind worthy the possessor of such a name, were the only inheritance of which he could boast.

In the year 1747, after having acquired such share of classical literature as the times he lived in would permit, O'Leary went to France, with the intention of devoting himself to the service of the Catholic Church.

A convent of Capuchin Friars at St. Malo in Brittany, was the school where O'Leary imbibed the principles of the learning, virtue, and philanthropy, which during a long life formed the prominent traits in his character. After having received holy orders, he continued to live in the monastery for some time.

In the year 1771 he returned to Ireland, and became resident in the city of Cork. Shortly after his arrival there, he contributed to the erection of a small chapel, in which he afterwards officiated, and which was generally known in Cork as "Father O'Leary's Chapel." Here he preached on the Sundays and principal festivals of the year to persons of different religious persuasions who crowded it to excess when it was known that he was to appear in the pulpit. His sermons were chiefly remarkable for a happy train of strong moral reasoning, bold figure, and scriptural allusion.

HIS CONTROVERSY WITH AN INFIDEL.

Some time in the year 1775, a book was published, the title of which was—"Thoughts on Nature and Religion," which contained much gross blasphemy. Its author, a Scottish physician of the name of Blair, residing in Cork, undertook to be the champion of free-thinking in religion; and, under the plausible pretext of vindicating the conduct of Servetus in his controversy with Calvin, this writer boldly attacked some of the most universally received articles of the Christian Creed. The work attracted some share of public attention. A poetical effusion in verse was addressed to Blair in reply by a minister of the Protestant Church; and an Anabaptist minister also entered the lists with a pamphlet nearly as sceptical as the one he professed to answer.

Father O'Leary's friends thought his style of controversy better suited to silence the Doctor than that of either of the tried opponents, and persuaded him to enter the lists. They were not disappointed. His reply crushed Blair; while his wit and logic and grand toleration raised him to the esteem and gratitude of his fellow-men. His first letter opens with this beautiful introduction:

"Sir—Your long expected performance has

at length made its appearance. If the work tended to promote the happiness of society, to animate our hopes, to subdue our passions, to instruct man in the happy science of purifying the pulluted recesses of a vitiated heart, to confirm him in his exalted notion of the dignity of his nature, and thereby to inspire him with sentiments averse to whatever may debase the excellence of his origin, the public would be indebted to you; your name would be recorded amongst the assertors of morality and religion; and I myself, though brought up in a different persuasion from yours, would be the first to offer my incense at the shrine of merit. But the tendency of your performance is to deny the divinity of Christ and the immortality of the soul. In denying the first, you sap the foundations of religion; you cut off at one blow the merit of our faith, the comfort of our hope, and the motives of our charity. In denying the immortality of the soul, you degrade human nature, and confound man with the vile and perishable insect. In denying both, you overturn the whole system of religion, whether natural or revealed; and in denying religion, you deprive the poor of the only comfort which supports them under their distresses and afflictions; you wrest from the hands of the powerful and rich the only bridle to their injustices and passions, and pluck from the hearts of the guilty the greatest check to their crimes—I mean this remorse of conscience which can never be the result of a handful of organized matter; this interior monitor, which makes us blush in the morning at the disorders of the foregoing night; which erects in the breast of the tyrant a tribunal superior to his power; and whose importunate voice upbraids a Cain in the wilderness with the murder of his brother, and a Nero in his palace with that of his mother."

Deploring the folly of him who thinks "his soul is no more than a subtile vapor, which in death is to be breathed out in the air," he holds that such a person should "conceal his horrid belief with more secrecy than the Druids concealed their mysteries. * * In doing otherwise, the infidel only brings disgrace on himself; for the notion of religion is so deeply impressed on our minds, that the bold champions who would fain destroy it, are considered by the generality of mankind as public pests, spreading disorder and mortality wherever they appear; and in our feelings we discover the delusions of cheating philosophy, which can never introduce a religion more pure than that of the Christian, nor confer a more glorious privilege on man than that of an immortal soul."

HIS INTERVIEW WITH DR. MANN.

Before he entered into a controversy with Doctor Blair, he deemed it prudent, owing to the state of sufferance in which Catholic priests then lived in Ireland, to obtain the sanction of the Protestant bishop of the diocese. To this end he waited on Doctor Mann at the episcopal palace. The interview is said to have been humorous in the extreme. O'Leary's figure, joined to an originality of manner, sterling wit, and an imagination which gave a color to every object on which it played, made him a visitor of no common kind; and as the bishop was not cast in the mould of "handsome orthodoxy," the meeting was long remembered by both parties. After some explanation, Doctor Mann gave his consent to the undertaking; in consequence of which the public were soon gratified by the appearance of his letters to Blair, whose discomfiture was so complete that he never wrote a public letter afterwards.

CONTROVERSY WITH JOHN WESLEY.

Wesley published in January, 1786, what he called, "A Letter containing the Civil Principles of Roman Catholics;" also, "a Defence of the Protestant Association." In these letters he maintained that Papists "ought not to be tolerated by any government—Protestant, Mohometan, or Pagan." In support of this doctrine, he says—

"Again, those who acknowledge the spiritual power of the Pope, can give no security of their allegiance to any government; but all Roman Catholics acknowledge this: therefore they can give no security for their allegiance."

In support of this line of argument, he treated his readers to this bit of lively information:—

"But it might be objected, 'nothing dangerous to English liberty is to be apprehended from them.' I am not so certain of that. Some time since a Romish priest came to one I know, and after talking with her largely, broke out, 'You are no heretic; you have the experience of a real Christian.' 'And would you,' she asked, 'burn me alive?' He said, 'God forbid! unless it were for the good of the Church.'"

In noticing which Father O'Leary humorously replies—

"A priest then said to a woman, whom Mr. Wesley *knows*, 'I see you are no heretic; you have the experience of a real Christian.' 'And would you burn me?' says she. 'God forbid!' replied the priest, 'except for the good of the Church!' Now, this priest must be descended from some of those who attempted to blow up a river with gunpowder, in order to drown a city. Or he must have taken her for a witch, whereas, by his own confession, she 'was no heretic.' A gentleman whom *I know* declared to me, upon his honor, that he heard Mr. Wesley repeat, in a sermon preached by him in the city of Cork, the following words: 'A little bird cried out in Hebrew, O Eternity! Eternity! who can tell the length of Eternity?' I am, then, of opinion that a *litttle Hebrew bird* gave Mr. Wesley the important information about the priest and the woman. One story is as interesting as the other, and both are equally alarming to the Protestant interest."

Alluding to the statute of Henry VI, which

bound every Englishman of the Pale to shave his upper lip, or clip his whiskers, to distinguish himself from an Irishman, he says: "It had tended more to their mutual interest, and the glory of that monarch's reign, not to go to the nicety of *splitting a hair*, but encourage the growth of their *fleeces*, and inspire them with such mutual love for each other as to induce them to kiss one another's beards, as brothers salute each other at Constantinople, after a few days' absence. I am likewise of opinion that Mr. Wesley, who prefaces his letter with 'the interest of the Protestant religion,' would reflect more honor on his ministry in promoting the happiness of the people, by preaching love and union, than in widening the breach, and increasing their calamities by division. The English and Irish were, at that time, of the same religion, but, divided in their affections, were miserable. Though divided in speculative opinions, if united in sentiment, we would be happy. The English settlers breathed the vital air in England before they inhaled the soft breezes of our temperate climate. The present generation can say, 'Our fathers and grandfathers have been born, bred, and buried here. We are Irishmen, as the descendants of the Normans who have been born in England are Englishmen.'

"Thus, born in an island in which the ancients might have placed their Hesperian gardens and golden apples, the temperature of the climate, and the quality of the soil inimical to poisonous insects, have cleansed our veins from the sour and acid blood of the Scythians and Saxons. We begin to open our eyes, and to learn wisdom from the experience of ages. We are tender-hearted; we are good-natured; we have feelings. We shed tears on the urns of the dead; deplore the loss of hecatcombs of victims slaughtered on gloomy altars of religious bigotry; cry on seeing the ruins of cities over which fanaticism has displayed the funeral torch; and sincerely pity the blind zeal of our Scotch and English neighbors, whose constant character is to pity none, for erecting the banners of persecution at a time when the Inquisition is abolished in Spain and Milan, and the Protestant gentry are caressed at Rome, and live unmolested in the luxuriant plains of France and Italy.

"The statute of Henry VI is now grown obsolete. The razor of calamity has shaved our lower and upper lips, and given us smooth faces. Our land is uncultivated; our country a desert; our natives are forced into the service of foreign kings, storming towns, and in the very heat of slaughter tempering Irish courage with Irish mercy. All our misfortunes flow from long-reigning intolerance and the storms which, gathering first in the Scotch and English atmosphere, never failed to burst over our heads.

"We are too wise to quarrel about religion. The Roman Catholics sing their psalms in Latin, with a few inflections of the voice. Our Protestant neighbors sing the same psalms in English, on a larger scale of musical notes. We never quarrel with our honest and worthy neighbors, the Quakers, for not singing at all; nor shall we ever quarrel with Mr. Wesley for raising his voice to heaven, and warbling forth his canticles on whatever tune he pleases, whether it be the tune of 'Guardian Angels' or 'Langolee.' We love social harmony, and in civil music hate discordance. Thus, when we go to the shambles, we never inquire into the butcher's religion, but into the quality of his meat. We care not whether the ox was fed in the Pope's territories, or on the mountains of Scotland, provided the joint be good; for though there be many heresies in old books, we discover neither heresy nor superstition in beef or claret. We divide them cheerfully with one another; and though of different religions, we sit over the bowl with as much cordiality as if we were at a love-feast."

He concludes with the following remarkable paragraph, in which humor, eloquence, and philanthropy, are happily blended—a paragraph worthy the Honorary Chaplain of the Irish Brigade;—

"We have obtained of late the privilege of planting tobacco in Ireland, and tobacconists want paper. Let Mr. Wesley then come with me, as the curate and barber went to shave and bless the library of Don Quixote. All the old books, old canons, sermons, and so forth, tending to kindle feuds, or promote rancor, let us fling out at the windows. Society will lose nothing: the tobacconists will benefit by the spoils of antiquity. And if, upon mature deliberation we decree that Mr. Wesley's 'Journal,' and his apology for the Association's 'Appeal,' should share the same fate with the old buckrams, we will procure them a gentle fall. After having rocked ourselves in the large and hospitable cradle of the *Free Press*, where the peer and the commoner, the priest and the alderman, the friar and the swaddler,* can stretch themselves at full length, provided they be not too churlish, let us laugh at those who breed useless quarrels, and set to the world the bright example of toleration and benevolence. A peaceable life and happy death to all Adam's children! May the ministers of religion of every denomination, whether they pray at the head of their congregations in embroidered vestments or black gowns, short coats, grey locks, powdered wigs, or black curls, instead of inflaming the rabble, and inspiring their hearers with hatred and animosity to their fellow-creatures, recommend love, peace, and harmony."

MEETING OF O'LEARY AND WESLEY.

"In a short time after this controversy had concluded, the parties met at the house of a mutual friend. Their different publications were mentioned; but kindness and sincere good feeling towards each other softened down the asperities of sectarian repulsiveness; and after an evening spent in a manner highly entertaining

* The name by which Methodists are known in Ireland.

and agreeable, they parted, each expressing his esteem for the other, and both giving the example, that public difference on a religious or political subject is quite consistent with the exercise of the duties of personal kindness and esteem. Wesley is said, in this instance, to have relaxed into a most agreeable companion; and O'Leary, by his wit, archness, and information, was an inexhaustible source of delight, entertainment, and instruction."

DR. O'LEARY AND FATHER CALLANAN.

Dr. O'Leary, though with great talents for a controversialist, always sedulously avoided the angry theme of religious disputation. Once, however, notwithstanding his declared aversion to polemics, he was led into a controversy. While he was at Cork, he received a letter through the Post Office, the writer of which, in terms expressive of the utmost anxiety, stated that he was a clergyman of the established church, on whose mind impressions favorable to the Catholic Creed had been made by some of O'Leary's sermons. The writer then professing his enmity to angry controversy, wished to seek further information on some articles of the Catholic creed. His name he forbore to reveal. O'Leary, anxious to propagate the doctrine of his Church, replied in a manner perfectly satisfactory to his anonymous correspondent. Other doubts were expressed, and dissipated, until the correspondence had extended to eight or ten long letters.

O'Leary, in joy at his supposed triumph, whispered the important secret to a few ecclesiastical confidants; among whom was his bosom friend, the Rev. Lawrence Callanan, a Francisan friar, of Cork. Their congratulations and approbation were not wanting, to urge forward the champion of orthodoxy. His arguments bore all before them; even the obtacles arising from family and legal notions, were disregarded by the enthusiastic convert, and he besought O'Leary to name a time and place, at which he might lift the mysterious vizor by which he had hitherto been concealed; and above all, have an opportunity of expressing his gratitude to his friend and teacher.

The appointed hour arrived. O'Leary arranged his orthodox wig, put on his Sunday suit of sable, and sallied forth with all collected gravity of a man fully conscious of the novelty and responsibility of the affair in which he was engaged. He arrived at the appointed place of meeting some minutes after the fixed time, and was told that a respectable clergyman awaited his arrival in an adjoining parlor. O'Leary enters the room, where he finds, sitting at the table, with the whole correspondence before him, his brother friar, Lawrence Callanan, who, either from an eccentric freak, or from a wish to call O'Leary's controversial powers into action, had thus drawn him into a lengthened correspondence. The joke, in O'Leary's opinion, however, was carried too far, and it required the sacrifice of the correspondence and the interference of mutual friends, to effect a reconciliation.

O'LEARY AND THE QUAKERS.

In his "Plea for Liberty of Conscience," Father O'Leary pays the fellowing high tribute to that sect :—

"The Quakers," said he, "to their eternal credit, and to the honor of humanity, are the only persons who have exhibited a meekness and forbearance, worthy the imitation of those who have entered into a covenant of mercy by their baptism.

William Penn, the great Legislator of that people, had the success of a conqueror in establishing and defending his colony amongst savage tribes, without ever drawing the sword; the goodness of the most benevolent rulers in treating his subjects as his own children; and the tenderness of a universal father, who opened his arms to all mankind without distinction of sect or party. In his republic, it was not the religious creed but personal merit, that entitled every member of society to the protection and emoluments of the State. Rise from your grave, great man! and teach those sovereigns who make their subjects miserable on account of their catechisms, the method of making them happy. They! whose dominions resemble enormous prisons, where one part of the creation are distressed captives, and the other their unpitying keepers."

HIS RECEPTION AT THE ROTUNDO BY THE VOLUNTEERS.

"It was impossible that the high and distinguished claims to respect and esteem which O'Leary possessed, should escape unoticed by the Volunteer association. Never was a more glorious era in the history of Ireland, than whilst the wealth, valor, and genius of her inhabitants became combined for the welfare of their country—whilst every citizen was a soldier, and every paltry political or sectarian difference and distinction was lost in the full glow and fervor of the great constitutional object, which roused the energies and fixed the attention of the people. It was a spectacle worthy the proudest days of Greece or Rome; but it passed away like the sudden gleam of a summer sun. O'Leary was exceeded by none of his contemporaries as a patriot: but, though the coarse and misshapen habit of a poor friar of the order of St. Francis forebade his intrusion into the more busy scene of national politics, his pen was not inactive in enlightening and directing his countrymen in their constitutional pursuits. A highly respectable body of the Volunteers, the *Irish Brigade*, conferred on him the honorary dignity of Chaplain; and many of the measures discussed at the National Convention held in Dublin, had been previously submitted to his consideration and judgment. On the 11th of November, 1783, the same day on which the message said to be from Lord Kenmare was read at the National Convention, then holding its meetings in the Rotundo, Father O'Leary visited that celebrated assemblage. At his arrival at the outer door, the entire guard of the Volunteers received him under a full salute, and rested arms: he was ushered into the meeting amidst the cheers of the assembled delegates; and in the course of the debate which followed, his name was mentioned in the most flattering and complimenting manner, by most of the speakers. On his journey from Cork to the Capital on that occasion, his arrival had been anticipated in Kilkenny, where he remained to dine; and in consequence, the street in which the hotel at which he stopped was situate, was filled from an early hour with persons of every class, who sought to pay a testimony of respect to an individual, whose writings had so powerfully tended to promote the welfare and happiness of his countrymen."

O'LEARY AND JOHN O'KEEFE.

In the *Recollections of John O'Keefe*, the following anecdote is related :—

"In 1775 I was in company with Father O'Leary, at the house of Flynn, the printer in

Cork. O'Leary had a fine smooth brogue; his learning was extensive, and his wit brilliant. He was tall and thin, with a long, pale, and pleasant visage, smiling and expressive. His dress was an entire suit of brown, of the old shape; a narrow stock, tight about his neck; his wig amply powdered, with a high poking foretop. In the year, 1791, my son Tottenham and I met him in St. James's Park, (London,) at the narrow entrance near Spring Gardens. A few minutes after, we were joined accidentally by Jemmy Wilder, well known in Dublin—once the famous Macheath, in Smock Alley—a worthy and respectable character, of a fine, bold, athletic figure, but violent and extravagant in his mode of acting. He had quitted the stage, and commenced picture-dealer; and when we met him in the Park, was running after a man, who, he said, had bought a picture of Rubens for three shillings and sixpence at a broker's stall in Drury-lane, and which was to make his (Wilder's) fortune. Our loud laughing at O'Leary's jokes, and his Irish brogue, and our stopping up the pathway, which is here very narrow, brought a crowd about us. O'Leary was very fond of the drama, and delighted in the company of the 'Glorious Boys,' as he called the actors—particularly that of Johnny Johnstone, for his fine singing in a room."

O'LEARY AND THE IRISH PARLIAMENT.

On the 26th February, 1782, the following interesting debate took place, the subject under consideration being a clause in the Catholic Bill directed against the friars:—

"Sir Lucius O'Brien said, he did not approve of the regulars, though his candor must acknowledge that many men amongst them have displayed great abilities. Ganganelli (Clement XIV) and the Reverend Doctor Arthur O'Leary are distinguished among the Franciscans; and many great men have been produced in the Benedictine order. He saw no temptation that regulars had for coming here, if it was not to abandon certain competence where they were, for certain poverty in this kingdom.

"Mr. Grattan said, he could not hear the name of Father O'Leary mentioned without paying him that tribute of acknowledgment so justly due to his merit. At the time that this very man lay under the censure of a law which, in his own country, made him subject to transportation or death, from religious distinctions; and at the time that a prince of his own religion threatened this country with an invasion, this respectable character took up his pen, and unsolicited, and without a motive but that of real patriotism, to urge his own communion to a disposition of peace, and to support the law which had sentenced him to transportation. A man of learning—a philosopher—a Franciscan—did the most eminent service to his country in the hour of its greatest danger. He brought out a publication that would do honor to the most celebrated name. The whole kingdom must bear witness to its effect, by the reception they gave it. Poor in everything but genius and philosophy, he had no property at stake, no family to fear for; but descending from the contemplation of wisdom, and abandoning the ornaments of fancy, he humanely undertook the task of conveying duty and instruction to the lowest class of the people. If I did not know him (continued Mr. Grattan) to be a Christian clergyman, I should suppose him by his works to be a philosopher of the Augustine age. The regulars are a harmless body of men, and should not be disturbed.

"Mr. St. George declared, notwithstanding his determined opposition to the regulars, he would, for the sake of one exalted character of their body, be tolerant to the rest. But he, at the same time, would uniformly oppose the tolerating any more regular clergy than what were at present in the kingdom.

"Mr. Yelverton said, that he was proud to call such a man as Dr. O'Leary his particular friend. His works might be placed upon a footing with the finest writers of the age. They originated from the urbanity of the heart; because unattached to the world's affairs, he could have none but the purest motives of rendering service to the cause of morality and his country. Had he not imbibed every sentiment of toleration before he knew Father O'Leary, he should be proud to adopt sentiments of toleration from him. He should yield to the sense of the committee in respect to the limitation of regulars; because, he believed, no invitation which could be held out would bring over another O'Leary."

"In a more advanced stage of the Catholic

Bill, on the 5th of March, these eulogies gave rise to some words between 'the rival orators,' as Messrs. Flood and Grattan were then designated in parliament. 'I am not,' said Flood towards the end of a speech, 'the missionary of a religion I do not profess; nor do I speak eulogies on characters I will not imitate.' No challenge of this nature ever was given by either of these great men in vain. Mr. Grattan spoke at some length to the subject under debate, and concluded in these words: 'Now, one word respecting Dr. O'Leary. Something has been said about eulogies pronounced, and missionaries of religion. I am not ashamed of the part which I took in that gentleman's panegyric; nor shall I ever think it a disgrace to pay the tribute of praise to the philosopher and the virtuous man.'"

HIS INTERVIEW WITH DANIEL DANSER.

Father O'Leary, when in London, had a great desire to see Daniel Danser; but finding access to the king of misers very difficult, invented a singular plan to gain his object. He sent a message to the miser, to the effect that he had been in the Indies, become acquainted with a man of immense wealth named Danser, who had died intestate, and, without a shadow of doubt, was a relative of his. It may be that a recent dream, coupled with the troubled state of the palm of his right hand, had their share in inducing Daniel to allow the witty friar into his apartment. Once entered, O'Leary contrived to sit down without depriving Mr. Danser of the least portion of his dust, which seemed to please him much; for Daniel held that cleaning furniture was an invention of the enemy; that it only helped to wear it out; consequently, regarded his dust as the protector of his household gods. Daniel's fond dreams of wealth from the Indies being dispelled, O'Leary began to console him by an historical review of the Danser family, whose genealogy he traced from David, who *danced* before the Israelites, down to the Welsh *jumpers*, then contemporaries of *dancing* notoriety. His wit triumphed: for a moment the sallow brow of avarice became illumined by the indications of a delighted mind, and *Danser* had courage enough to invite his visitor to partake of a glass of wine, which, he said, he would procure for his refreshment. A cordial shake hands was the return made for O'Leary's polite refusal of so expensive a compliment; and he came from the house followed by its strange tenant, who, to the amusement of O'Leary, and the astonishment of the only other person who witnessed the scene, solicited the favor of another visit."

A FOP.

"The "two-edged sword of wit," as that faculty has been termed, was wielded by O'Leary in the more serious circumstances of life, as well as in its playful hours. An instance where the painful exercise of this was happily spared, occurred at one of the meetings of the English Catholics, during the celebrated *Blue Book* Controversy. One of the individuals who was expected to advocate the objectionable designation of "protesting Catholic dissenters," an appellation equally ludicrous and unnecessary, was remarkable for an affected mode of public speaking. What in dress is termed *foppish*, would be appropriate as applied to his oratory. He was no admirer of O'Leary, and the feeling of dislike was as mutual as could well be conceived. Him, therefore, O'Leary selected as the opponent with whom he meant to grapple. Those to whom he communicated his intention, and who knew his powers, looked forward with expectation "on tiptoe" for a scene of enjoyment that no anticipation could exaggerate. Disappointment was, however, their lot. The meeting passed over quietly, and neither the objectionable matter nor speaker was brought forward. However much his friends regretted this circumstance, O'Leary was himself sincerely pleased; for he never desired to give unnecessary pain. The gentlemen in concert with whom he acted, dined together after the meeting, and the conversation happening to turn on the disappointment which they had experienced in the result of the debate, one of them who knew O'Leary intimately, inquired what line of argument he had intended to pursue, if the meeting had assumed the objectionable aspect which was dreaded—this was applying the torch to gunpowder: he commenced an exhibition of the ludicrous so like what would have taken place, so true in manner and matter to what every one who knew the parties could anticipate, that the assemblage was convulsed with laughter to a degree that made it memorable in the recollections of all who witnessed it."

HIS PERSON AND MODE OF ARGUMENT.

Mr. Butler, in his Historical Memoirs, describes O'Leary's person and mode of argument thus:—

"The appearance of Father O'Leary was simple. In his countenance there was a mixture of goodness, solemnity, and drollery, which fixed every eye that beheld it. No one was more generally loved or revered; no one less assuming or more pleasing in his manner. Seeing his external simplicity, persons with whom he was arguing were sometimes tempted to treat him cavalierly; but then the solemnity with which he would mystify his adversary, and ultimately lead him into the most distressing absurdity was one of the most delightful scenes that conversation ever exhibited."

O'LEARY AND "CAPTAIN ROCK."

In Tom Moore's "Memoirs of Captain Rock," the outlaw gives the following humorous sketch:—

"The appearance of Father Arthur at our little chapel was quite unexpected. We had heard, indeed, that he was proceeding through distant parts of the country, but we had no idea that he would pay us a visit. The mind of man is a strange compound of opposite passion. I had everything to apprehend from the poor friar's preaching; yet, strange as it may appear, I was almost willing to have all my bright scenes overturned, provided I could have the pleasure to see and hear the celebrated Father O'Leary. He opposed our designs, disapproved of our motives, and censured our intentions; yet without having ever seen him, we loved—almost adored him. Fame had wafted his name even to Rockglen; and how could we but venerate a man who had exalted the character of Irishmen, vindicated our oppressed country, and obtained from the ranks of Protestantism, friends for our insulted creed.

"Besides, he was peculiarly adapted to our taste. He made the world laugh at the foibles of our enemies, and put us in good humor with ourselves. It was not, therefore, without some slight satisfaction that we were informed from the altar that the good friar meant to address us on our manifold transgressions. Never did men manifest such eagerness to receive reproof. At the sound of his name, there was a general rush towards the altar. The old women, for the first time in their lives, ceased coughing, and the old men desisted from spitting. The short people were elevated on their toes, and the tall people suffered their hats (felt ones) to be crushed as flat as pancakes, sooner then incommode their neighbors—a degree of politeness seldom practised in more polished assemblies. All breathed short and thick; and much as we venerated our good priest, we fancied he was particularly tedious in the lecture he thought fit to read us on our neglecting to go to confession, and on our dilatoriness in paying the last Easter dues. At length he concluded by announcing Father O'Leary."

LOTS DRAWN TO HAVE HIM AT DINNER

In 1779, O'Leary visited Dublin on business connected with a bill before parliament, which aimed at the destruction of the friars. During his visit to Dublin, at this period, the following circumstance, quite characteristic of O'Leary, is said to have taken place. He accidentally met, in the lobby of the House of Commons, the late Lord Avonmore, then Mr. Yelverton, and two gentlemen, members of the legislature; who, on his appearance, entered into a friendly altercation to determine with which of them O'Leary should, on the next day, share the splendid hospitality which reigned in the metropolis during the sessions of parliament. It was at length decided that the prize of his unrivalled wit and sociability should be determined by lot. O'Leary was an amused and silent spectator of the contest. The fortunate winner was congratulated on his success; and the rivals separated to meet on the morrow.

When the hour of dinner was come, O'Leary forgot which of his three friends was to be his host. It was too late to make formal inquiries; and, as he was the honored guest, he dared not absent himself. In this difficulty, his ready imagination suggested an expedient. His friends, he recollected, lived in the same square, and he therefore, some short time after the usual dinner hour, sent a servant to inquire at each of the houses—'if Father O'Leary was there?' At the two first, where application was made, the reply was in the negative; but at the last, the porter answered, that 'he was not there; but that dinner was ordered to be kept back, as he was every moment expected.' Thus directed, 'Father Arthur's' apology for delay was a humorous and detailed account of his expedient—the evening flew quickly away on the wings of eloquence and wit, and the laughable incident was long remembered and frequently repeated."

Father O'Leary's great intimacy with the leading Protestants of London, gave rise to a rumor that he, like Lord Dunboyne and Mr. Kirwin, had read his recantation. He contradicts it in the following letter:— "*London, June* 5, 1790.

"SIR—A confusion of names gave rise, some months ago, to a mistake copied from the *Dublin Evening Post* into the *Bath Chronicle*, and other papers in this kingdom, viz., that 'I had read my recantation in St. Werburgh's church in Dublin.' Thus a mistake has changed me into a conformist, though I never changed my creed.

"If in reality the tenets of my Church were such as prejudice and ignorance proclaim them:—if they taught me that a papal dispensation could sanctify guilt, sanction conspiracies, murders, the extirpation of my fellow-creatures on account of difference of religious opinions, perjury to promote the Catholic cause, by pious breaches of allegiance to Protestant kings, or rebellion against their government;—if it were an article of my belief that a priestly absolution without sorrow for my sins, or a resolution of amendment, had the power of a charm to reclaim me to the state of unoffending infancy, and enable me, like Milton's devil, to leap from the gulf of sin into paradise without purifying my heart or changing my affections;—if it were an article of my faith that the grace of an indulgence could give me the extraordinary privilege of sinning without guilt or offending without punishment;—if it inculcated any maxim evasive of moral rectitude:—in a word, if the features of my religion corresponded with the pictures drawn of it in flying pamphlets and anniversary declamations, I would consider myself and the rest of my fraternity as downright idiots, wickedly stupid, to remain one hour in a state which deprives us of our rights as citizens, whereas such an accommodating scheme would make them not only attainable, but certain.

"Your correspondent does me the honor to rank me with Lord Dunboyne, formerly titular Bishop of Cork, and with Mr. Kirwan. If they have changed their religion from a thorough conviction of its falsehood, they have done well. It is the duty of every sincere admirer after truth to comply with the immediate dictates of his conscience, in embracing that religion which he believes most acceptable to God. Deplorable, indeed, must be the state of the man who lives in wilful error. For, however an all-wise God may hereafter dispose of those who err in their honesty, and whose error is involuntary and invincible, surely no road can be right to the wretch who walks in it against conviction. A thorough conviction, then, that I am in the right road to eternal life, if my moral conduct corresponds with my speculative belief, keeps me within the pale of my Church in direct opposition to my temporal interest; and no Protestant nobleman or gentleman of my acquaintance esteems me the less for adhering to my creed, knowing that a Catholic and an honest man are not contradictory terms.

"I do not consider Lord Dunboyne as a model after whom I should copy. With his silver locks, and at an age when persons who had devoted themselves to the service of the altar in their early days, should, like the Emperor Charles V, rather think of their coffins than the nuptial couch, that prelate married a young woman. Whether the glowing love of truth or Hymen's torch induced him to change the Roman Pontifical for the Book of Common Prayer, and the psalms he and I often sang together for a bridal hymn, his own conscience is the most competent to determine: certain however, it is, that, if the charms of the fair sex can captivate an old bishop to such a degree as to induce him to renounce his Breviary, similar motives, and the prospect of aggrandizement, may induce a young ecclesiastic to change his cassock.

"Having from my early days accustomed myself to get the mastery over ambition and love—the two passions that in every age have enslaved the greatest heroes—your correspondent may rest assured that I am not one of the trio mentioned in this letter.—Arthur O'Leary."

O'LEARY AND THE RECTOR.

A Protestant rector invited O'Leary to see his parish church, a building remarkable for its architectural beauty. While the friar was viewing the building, the rector thought he was contrasting its nakedness with the interior beauty of the Roman Catholic churches, and observed:

"You perceive, Mr. O'Leary," said he, "that, different from you, we are very sparing of ornaments in our churches; we have neither paintings nor statuary to attract the worshipper's attention." "Ah!" replied O'Leary, with an arch smile, "you are *young housekeepers*, you know."

LADY MORGAN.

Lady Morgan, in her "Wild Irish Girl," speaking of "Father John," chaplain of the Prince of Coolavin, says:—"Father John was modelled on the character of the Dean of Sligo, Dr. Flynn, one of those learned, liberal, and accomplished gentlemen of the Irish Catholic hierarchy of that day, whom foreign travel and education, and consequent intercourse with European society and opinions, sent back to Ireland for its advantage and illustration, thus turning the penalties of its shallow and jealous government into a national benefit. At the head of this distinguished order stood the illustrious Father O'Leary, the Catholic Dean Swift of his time, the champion of peace, and the eloquent preacher of Christian charity. His noble works live to attest his fitness to counsel his country for her good, while his brilliant wit kept up her reputation for that splendid gift which penal statutes can neither give nor take away."

A BATCH OF INTERESTING ANECDOTES.

In his "Personal Sketches," Sir Jonah Barrington gives us a portrait of Father O'Leary:—

"I frequently had an opportunity of meeting at my father-in-law Mr. Grogan's, where he often dined, a most worthy priest, Father O'Leary, and have listened frequently, with great zest, to anecdotes which he used to tell with a quaint yet spirited humor, quite unique. His manner, his air, his countenance, all bespoke wit, talent, and a good heart. I liked his company excessively, and have often regretted I did not cultivate his acquaintance more, or recollect his witticisms better. It was singular, but it was a fact, that even before Father O'Leary opened his lips, a stranger would say, 'That is an Irishman,' and, at the same time, guess him to be a priest.

"One anecdote in particular I remember. Coming from St. Omers, he told us, he stopped a few days to visit a brother-priest in the town of

Boulogne-sur-Mer. Here he heard of a great curiosity, which all people were running to see—a curious bear that some fishermen had taken at sea out of a wreck; it had sense, and attempted to utter a sort of *lingo*, which they called *patois*, but which nobody understood.

"O'Leary gave his six sous to see the wonder which was shown at the port by candle-light, and was a very odd kind of animal, no doubt. The bear had been taught a hundred tricks, all to be performed at the keeper's word of command. It was late in the evening when O'Leary saw him, and the bear seemed sulky; the keeper, however, with a short spike fixed at the end of a pole, made him move about briskly. He marked on sand what o'clock it was, with his paw; and distinguished the men and women in a very comical way: in fact, our priest was quite diverted. The beast at length grew tired—the keeper hit him with the pole—he stirred a little, but continued quite sullen; his master coaxed him—no! he would not work! At length, the brute of a keeper gave him two or three sharp pricks with the goad, when he roared out most tremendously, and rising on his hind-legs, swore at his tormentors in very good native Irish. O'Leary waited no longer, but went immediately to the mayor, whom he informed that the blackguard fishermen had sewed up a poor Irishman in a bear's-skin, and were showing him about for six sous! The civic dignitary, who had himself seen the bear, would not believe our friend. At last, O'Leary prevailed on him to accompany him to the room. On their arrival, the bear was still on duty, and O'Leary stepped up to him, says:—'*Cianos tha'n thu, a Phadhrig?*' (How d'ye do, Pat?) '*Slan, go raimh math agut!*' (Pretty well, thank you,) says the bear. The people were surprised to hear how plainly he spoke—but the mayor ordered him directly to be ripped up; and after some opposition, and a good deal of difficulty, Pat stepped forth stark naked out of the bear's-skin wherein he had been fourteen or fifteen days most cleverly stitched. The women made off—the men stood astonished—and the mayor ordered his keepers to be put in goal unless they satisfied him; but that was presently done. The bear afterwards told O'Leary that he was very well fed, and did not care much about the clothing; only they worked him too hard: the fishermen had found him at sea on a hencoop, which had saved him from going to the bottom, with a ship wherein he had a little venture of dried cod from Dungarvan, and which was bound from Waterford to Bilboa. He could not speak a word of any language but Irish, and had never been at sea before: the fishermen had brought him in, fed him well, and endeavored to repay themselves by showing him as a curiosity.

"O'Leary's mode of telling this story was quite admirable. I never heard any anecdote (and I believe this one to be true) related with such genuine drollery, which was enhanced by his not changing a muscle himself, while every one of his hearers was in a paroxysm of laughter.

"Another anecdote he used to tell with incomparable dramatic humor. By the bye, all his stories were somehow national; and this gives me occasion to remark, that I think Ireland is, at this moment, as little known in many parts of the Continent as it seems to have been then. I have myself heard it more than once spoken of as an *English town.* At Nancy, where Father O'Leary was travelling, his native country happened to be mentioned when one of the party, a quiet French farmer of Burgundy, asked, in an unassuming tone, '*If Ireland stood encore?*' 'Encore,' said an astonished John Bull, a courier coming from Germany—'encore! to be sure she does; we have her yet, I assure you, monsieur.' 'Though neither very safe, nor very sound,' interposed an officer of the Irish Brigade, who happened to be present, looking very significantly at O'Leary, and not very complacently at the courier. 'And pray, monsieur,' rejoined John Bull to the Frenchman, 'why *encore?*' '*Pardon, monsieur,*' replied the Frenchman, 'I heard it had been worn out (*fatigue*) long ago, by the great number of people that were living in it.' The fact is, the Frenchman had been told, and really understood, that Ireland was a large house, where the English were wont to send their idle vagabonds, and from whence they were drawn out again, as they were wanted, to fill the ranks of the army."

A DOG'S RELIGION.

One day, while walking in the suburbs of the city of Cork, he met the Rev. Mr. Flack, a Protestant clergyman, and Mr. Solomons, a Jew —both friends of his. Mr. Flack's dog was runing on before them. "Good morrow, friends," said O'Leary. "Well, what interesting topic engages your attention now?" "To be candid with you," replied the clergyman, "we were just conjecturing what religion this dog of mine would be likely to embrace, if it were possible for him to choose." "Strange subject, indeed," said O'Leary; "but were I to offer an opinion, I would venture to say he would become a Protestant!" "How," asked the Protestant clergyman and the Jew. "Why," replied O'Leary, "he would not be a Jew, for, you know, he would retain his passion for pork: he would not become a Catholic, for I am quite certain he would eat meat on a Friday. What religion, then, could he become, but a Protestant!"

HOWARD, THE PHILANTHROPIST, AND MR. HENRY SHEARS.

"About this time it was," says his biographer, "that the philanthropist Howard, led by his benevolent enthusiasm to fathom dungeons, vindicate the wrongs, and alleviate the sufferings of the lonely and forgotten victim of vice and crime, arrived at Cork. A society had for some years existed in that city 'for the relief and discharge of persons confined for small debts,' of which O'Leary was an active and conspicuous member. This association had its origin in the humane mind of Henry Shears, Esq., the father of two distinguished victims to the political distractions of their country in 1798: and a literary production of that gentleman, which in its style and matter emulated the elegance and morality of Addison, strengthened and matured the benevolent institution. During Mr. Howard's stay in Cork, he was introduced to O'Leary by their common friend, Archdeacon Austen. Two such minds required but an opportunity to admire and venerate each other; and frequently, in after times, Howard boasted of sharing the friendship and esteem of the friar."

HIS HABITS OF STUDY—HIS INFLUENCE.

"In the midst of the cares and distractions," says his biographer, "to which the active duties of the ministry subjected O'Leary, he still indulged his usual habits of study. No unexpected visitor ever found him unoccupied: his reading was extensive, profound, and incessant; and his hours of silence and retreat as many as he could abstract from the necessary and inevitable claim of his flock, or could deny to the kind importunity of his numerous and respectable acquaintance. Few men ever possessed the power of enjoying an extensive influence over public opinion more than O'Leary. Every thing he said or wrote was by every one admired. The wise and learned were delighted with the original and correct views which he took of every subject that employed his mind; whilst the amiable simplicity of his manners, the endearing kindness of his disposition, and the worth, purity, and uprightness of his life and conduct, were claims to regard that could neither be denied nor unattended to. It is, therefore, to be lamented that such trancendent faculties should have remained suspended or inactive, or been, for a moment, diverted in their application from their appropriate object or natural sphere—the moral correction of the age."

EDMOND BURKE.

On Father O'Leary's arrival in London he was anxiously sought after by his countrymen residing in that capital, who all felt gratified by every opportunity which offered itself, of paying respect to one who had done so much honor to religion and their country. Mr. Edmond Burke was very marked in the regard which he manifested to O'Leary. * * It was, in fact, impossible, after an evening spent in his society, not to seek at every future opportunity a renewal of the delight which his wit, pleasantry, and wisdom afforded.

HIS CHARITY.

Like Dean Swift, Father O'Leary relieved, every Monday morning, a number of reduced roomkeepers and working men. The average of his weekly charity amounted to two, sometimes three pounds—though he had no income except that derived from the contributions of those who frequented the poor Capuchin little chapel.

After the publication of his "Essay on Toleration," Father O'Leary was elected a member of the "Monks of St. Patrick," which took its rise under the auspices of that great lawyer, Lord Avonmore, then Mr. Yelverton. As a return for the honor thus conferred on him, he expressed his gratitude in the dedication of his various productions, which he collected together, and published in 1781.

At one of the meetings of the English Catholic Board, whilst O'Leary was addressing the chairman, the late Lord Petre, it was suggested by the noble president that the speaker was entering on topics not calculated to promote the unanimity of the assembly. O'Leary, however, persevered: on which Lord Petre interrupted him, adding, "Mr. O'Leary, I regret much to see that you are *out of order*." The reply was equally quick and characteristic—"I thank you for your anxiety, my lord; but I assure you *I never was in better health in my life*." The archness of manner with which these words were uttered was triumphant, and every unpleasant feeling was lost in the mirth which was necessarily excited.

O'LEARY VERSUS CURRAN.

In the "Reminiscences" of the celebrated singer and composer, Michael Kelly, the following interesting anecdotes are given: "I had the pleasure to be introduced to my worthy countryman, the Rev. Father O'Leary, the well-known Roman Catholic priest; he was a man of infinite wit, of instructing and amusing conversation. I felt highly honored by the notice of this pillar of the Roman Church; our tastes were congenial, for his reverence was mighty fond of whisky-punch, and so was I; and many a jug of Saint Patrick's eye-water, night after night, did his Reverence and myself enjoy, chatting over the exhilarating and national beverage. He sometimes favored me with his company at dinner; when he did, I always had a corned shoulder of mutton for him, for he, like some others of his countrymen who shall be nameless, was marvellously fond of that dish.

"One day the facetious John Philpot Curran, who was very partial to the said corned mutton, did me the honor to meet him. To enjoy the society of such men was an intellectual treat. They were great friends, and seemed to have a mutual respect for each other's talents and, as it may be easily imagined, O'Leary versus Curran was no bad match.

"One day, after dinner, Curran said to him, 'Reverend father, I wish you were Saint Peter.'

"'And why, Counsellor, would you wish that I were Saint Peter?' asked O'Leary.

"'Because, reverend father, in that case,' said Curran, 'you would have the keys of heaven, and you could *let me in.*'

"'By my honor and conscience, Counsellor,' replied the divine, 'it would be better for you if I had the keys of the other place, for then I could *let you out.*' Curran enjoyed the joke, which, he admitted, had a good deal of justice in it.

HIS TRIUMPH OVER DR. JOHNSON.

"O'Leary told us of a whimsical triumph which he once enjoyed over the celebrated Dr. Johnson. O'Leary was very anxious to be introdueed to that learned man, and Mr. Arthur Murphy took him one morning to the doctor's lodgings. On his entering the room, the doctor viewed him from top to toe, without taking any notice of him; and, at length, darting one of his sourest looks at him, he spoke to him in the Hebrew language, to which O'Leary made no reply. 'Why do you not answer me, sir?' 'Faith, sir,' said O'Leary, 'because I don't understand the language in which you are addressing me.' Upon this, the doctor, with a contemptuous sneer, said to Murphy, 'Why, sir, this is a pretty fellow you have brought hither. Sir, he does not comprehend the primitive language.' O'Leary immediately bowed very low, and complimented the doctor in a long speech in Irish, to which the doctor, not understanding a word, made no reply, but looked at Murphy. O'Leary, seeing the doctor was puzzled at hearing a language of which he was ignorant, said to Murphy, pointing to the doctor, 'This is a pretty fellow to whom you have brought me. Sir, he does not understand the language of the sister kingdom.' The reverend *padre* then made another low bow, and quitted the room."

A NOLLE PROSEQUI.

At the time that Barry Yelverton was Attorney-General, himself and O'Leary, while enjoying the beauties of Killarney, had the rare fortune to witness a staghunt. The hunted animal ran towards the spot where the Attorney-General and O'Leary stood. "Ah!" said Father Arthur, with genuine wit, "how naturally instinct leads him to come to you, that you may deliver him by a *nolle prosequi!*"

THE PRINCE OF WALES.

George the Fourth, when Prince of Wales, frequently had as guests at his table Sheridan, Grattan, Curran, Flood, and Father O'Leary. Croly, in his "Life of George the Fourth," says—"An occasional guest, and a sufficiently singular one, was an Irish Franciscan, Arthur O'Leary, a man of strong faculties and considerable knowledge. His first celebrity was as a pamphleteer, in a long battle with Woodward, the able Bishop of Cloyne, in Ireland. * * O'Leary abounded in Irish anecdote, and was a master of pleasant humor.

"Sheridan said that he considered claret the true parliamentary wine for the peerage, for it might make a man sleepy or sick, but it never warmed his heart, or stirred up his brains. Port, generous port, was for the Commons—it was for the business of life—it quickened the circulation and fancy together. For his part, he never felt that he spoke as he liked, until after a couple of bottles. O'Leary observed, that this was like a *porter;* he never could go steady without a *load* on his head."

THE CLOSING SCENES OF HIS LIFE.

"The disturbances," says his biographer, "by which Ireland was convulsed in 1798 pained O'Leary's mind. The efforts made by the tools of a base faction, to give the tinge of religious fanaticism to the political distractions of that country, excited his indignation; and, as his name had been wantonly and insultingly introduced by Sir Richard Musgrave, in his libellous compilation on the Irish Rebellions, he entertained the notion of publishing a refutation of the calumnies which had been so industriously circulated against the Catholics, not only in that scandalous work, but likewise in various other historical essays at that time. For this purpose O'Leary had prepared some very valuable manuscript collections: he looked back to the history of the earlier periods of the English rule in Ireland; and from his friends in various parts of that kingdom he procured authentic details of the insurrectionary disturbances: impartiality was his object; and he left no means untried to collect the most voluminous and exact account of every circumstance connected with, or immediately arising out of, the rebellion, the history of which he ultimately declared it his design to publish.

"The progress of disease, and the rapidly increasing infirmities of old age, hindered the fulfilment of O'Leary's wishes: he was unable to proceed into any part of the task of composition, but he was relieved from anxiety by the fortunate circumstance of his intimacy with Francis Plowden Esq., whose historical review of Ireland, and whose subsequent publication in defence of that country, have raised him to a rank amongst historians, honorably and deservedly conspicuous. When O'Leary learned that his friend was engaged, at the desire of Mr. Pitt, in writing the 'Historical Review,' he sent him his invaluable collections, as affording the best and most authentic materials for the recent history of Ireland; and the manner in which the documents, thus furnished, were applied to the purposes of truth, must have given gratification to O'Leary's mind, had he lived long enough to witness this successful vindication of his country and religion. His descent to the grave was too rapid to afford him that pleasure; and it was not till it had closed over his remains, that the world was gratified with the best and most authentic work ever published on the political history of Ireland.

"We approach now to the last scene of O'Leary's busy life; and it is one which, like too many others, preaches to mankind the necessity of being always prepared for the unrevealed hour that shall terminate mortal existence.

"Towards the end of the year 1801, ill health shed a gloom over his mind, to which the consciousness of approaching dissolution gave facilities and permanency. His contests with bad men had been frequent; and the frailities and follies of the world, and the instability of human friendship, which he had often experienced, haunted his mind at this time to a degree that was painful for those who loved and revered him, to witness. His medical friends tried the resources of their professional skill for the alleviation of his disease in vain; and as a last prescription, they recommended to him a short residence in the south of France, as calculated, if any thing could, to revive his spirits and restore his health. Agreeably to this advice, in company with Mr. M'Grath, a medical friend, to whose kindness he was much indebted, he proceeded to France; but his hopes of relief were disappointed, and he shortly determined on returning to London. The state in which he found society in France—so different from what it had been, when he first visited 'the lovely, fertile south,' shocked him; and he uttered his opinion of the change which he witnessed, by saying, emphatically, 'that there was not now a *gentleman* in all France.'

"His arrival in London was on the 7th of January, 1802. It was his intention to have landed at Dover; but tempestuous weather compelled the vessel in which he was to land at Ramsgate. The effects of this voyage tended to hasten his death, which took place the morning after his arrival in London, in the 73rd year of his age."

DANIEL O'CONNELL.

DARBY MORAN.

O'Connell in his celebrated speech in defence of the Rev. T. Maguire, relates the following story, in which the reader will not fail to perceive the little chance which perjury had in escaping his detection :—

"Allow me," said he, addressing the Court, "to tell you a story, which is not the worse for being perfectly true. I was assessor of the Sheriff at an election in the county of Clare; a freeholder came to vote under the name of Darby Moran, and as Darby Moran both his signature and mark were attached to the certificate of Registry. He, of course, was objected to. It was insisted that if he was illiterate, he could not have written his name—if literate, he should not have added his mark; in either view it was contended, with the vehemence suited to such occasions, that his registry was bad. It is, wherever I have authority to adjudicate, a rule with me to decide as few abstract propositions as I possibly can. I therefore resolved first to ascertain the fact whether Darby Moran could write or not. I accordingly gave him paper, and asked him could he write his name. He flippantly answered that he could, and in my presence instantly wrote down 'John O'Brien'— he totally forgot that he was playing Darby Moran. Thus this trick was exposed and defeated."

A DEAD MAN WITH LIFE IN HIM.

It was difficult for O'Connell, even at an advanced period of his professional career, to exhibit those powers as an advocate, which were afterwards so finely developed; for the silk gown that encased inferior merit gave a precedence to Protestant lawyers of even younger standing, and he rarely had an opportunity of addressing a jury. This probably induced him to cultivate with more ardor a talent for cross-examination, which was unquestionably unrivalled, and which was displayed by him at a very early period

It exhibited itself very strongly in a trial on the Munster Circuit, in which the question was, the validity of a will, by which property to some amount was devised, and which the plaintiffs alleged was forged. The subscribing witnesses swore that the deceased signed the will while *life was in him.*

The evidence was going strong in favor of the will—at last O'Connell undertook to cross-examine one of the witnesses. He shrewdly observed that he was particular in swearing several times that "life was in the testator when the will was signed," and that he saw his hand sign it.

"By virtue of your oath was he alive," said Mr. O'Connell.

"By virtue of my oath, *life was in him;*" and this the witness repeated several times.

"Now," continued O'Connell, with great solemnity, and assuming an air of inspiration—"I call on you, in presence of your Maker, before whom you must one day be judged for the evidence you give here to-day, I solemnly ask—and answer me at your peril—was it not a live fly that was in the dead man's mouth when his hand was placed on the will?"

'The witness fell instantaneously on his knees, and acknowledged it was so, and that the fly was placed in the mouth of deceased to enable the witnesses to swear *that life was in him.*

The intuitive quickness with which O'Connell conjectured the cause of the fellow's always swearing that "life was in him," obtained for him the admiration of every one in Court, and very materially assisted in securing his professional success.

A YOUNG JUDGE DONE.

In the course of his attendance at an Assizes in Cork, he was counsel in a case in which his client was capitally charged, and was so little likely to escape, and was actually so guilty of the crime, that his attorney considered the case utterly desperate.

O'Connell entered the Court aware of the hopelessness of his client's chances. He knew it was useless to attempt a defence in the ordinary way. There was evidence sufficient to ensure a conviction. At that time it happened that the present Chief Justice, then Sergeant, Lefroy presided, in the absence of one of the judges who had fallen ill. O'Connell understood the sort of man he had on the Bench. He opened the defence by putting to the first witness a number of the most illegal questions. He, of course, knew they were illegal, and that objections would be raised.

Sergeant Goold was the crown prosecutor, and he started up, and expressed his objections. The learned Chief Justice declared his concurrence, and decided peremptorily that he could not allow Mr. O'Connell to proceed with his line of examination.

"Well, then, my lord," said O'Connell, after a little expostulation, "as you refuse permitting me to defend my client, I leave his fate in your hands;" and he flung his brief from him, adding, as he turned away, "the blood of that man, my lord, will be on your head, if he is condemned." O'Connell then left the Court. In half-an-hour afterwards, as he was walking on the flagway outside, the attorney for the defence ran out to him without his hat. "Well," said O'Connell, "he is found guilty?" "No, sir," answered the solicitor, "he has been acquitted." O'Connell is said to have smiled meaningly on the occasion, as if he had anticipated the effect of the *ruse;* for it was a *ruse* he had recourse to, in order to save the unfortunate culprit's life. He knew that flinging the onus on a young and a raw judge could be the only chance for his client. The judge did take up the case O'Connell had ostensibly, in a pet, abandoned. The witnesses were successively cross-examined by the judge himself. He conceived a prejudice in favor of the accused. He, perhaps, had a natural timidity of incurring the responsibility thrown on him by O'Connell. He charged the jury in the prisoner's favor, and the consequence was, the unexpected acquittal of the prisoner. "*I knew*," said O'Connell afterwards, "the only chance was to throw the responsibility on the judge."

O'CONNELL AND A SNARLING ATTORNEY.

O'Connell could be seen to greatest advantage in an Irish court of justice. There he displayed every quality of the lawyer and the advocate. He showed perfect mastery of his profession, and he exhibited his own great and innate qualities. Who that ever beheld him on the Munster circuit, when he was in the height of his fame, but must have admired his prodigious versatility of formidable powers. His pathos was often admirable—his humor flowed without effort or art. What jokes he uttered!—what sarcasms! How well he worked his case, never throwing away a chance, never relaxing his untiring energies. How he disposed of a pugnacious attorney may be gathered from the following:—

"For a round volley of abusive epithets nobody could surpass him. One of his droll comic sentences was often worth a speech of an hour in putting down an opponent, or in gaining supporters to his side. At *Nisi Prius*, he turned his mingled talent for abuse and drollery to great effect. He covered a witness with ridicule, or made a cause so ludicrous, that the real grounds of complaint became invested with absurdity.

"One of the best things he ever said was in an assize-town on the Munster circuit. The attorney of the side opposite to that on which O'Connell was retained, was a gentleman remarkable for his combative qualities; delighted in being in a fight, and was foremost in many of the political scenes of excitement in his native town. His person was indicative of his disposition. His face was bold, menacing, and scornful in its expression. He had stamped on him the defiance and resolution of a pugilist. Upon either temple there stood erect a lock of hair, which no brush could smooth down. These locks looked like horns, and added to the combative expression of his countenance. He was fiery in his nature, excessively spirited, and ejaculated, rather than spoke to an audience; his speeches consisting of a series of short, hissing, spluttering sentences, by no means devoid of talent of a certain kind. Add to all this, that the gentleman was an Irish Attorney, and an Orangeman, and the reader may easily suppose that he was 'a character!'

Upon the occasion referred to, this gentleman gave repeated annoyance to O'Connell—by interrupting him in the progress of the cause—by speaking to the witnesses—and by interfering in a manner altogether improper, and unwarranted by legal custom. But it was no easy matter to make the combative attorney hold his peace—he, too, was an agitator in his own fashion. In vain did the counsel engaged with O'Connell in the cause sternly rebuke him; in vain did the judge admonish him to remain quiet; up he would jump, interrupting the proceedings, hissing out his angry remarks and vociferations with vehemence. While O'Connell was in the act of pressing a most important question he jumped up again, undismayed, solely for the purpose of interruption. O'Connell, losing all patience, suddenly turned round, and, scowling at the disturber, shouted in a voice of thunder—'Sit down, you audacious, snarling, pugnacious ram-cat.' Scarcely had the words fallen from his lips, when roars of laughter rang through the court. The judge himself laughed outright at the happy and humorous description of the combative attorney, who, pale with passion, gasped in inarticulate rage. The name of *ram-cat* struck to him through all his life."

HIS ENCOUNTER WITH BIDDY MORIARTY.

One of the drollest scenes of vituperation that O'Connell ever figured in took place in the early part of his life. Not long after he was called to the bar, his character and peculiar talents received rapid recognition from all who were even casually acquainted with him. His talent for vituperative language was perceived, and by some he was, even in those days, considered matchless as a scold.

There was, however, at that time in Dublin, a

certain woman, Biddy Moriarty, who had a huckster's stall on one of the quays nearly opposite the Four Courts. She was a virago of the first order, very able with her fist, and still more formidable with her tongue. From one end of Dublin to the other she was notorious for her powers of abuse, and even in the provinces Mrs. Moriarty's language had passed into currency. The dictionary of Dublin slang had been considerably enlarged by her, and her voluble impudence had almost become proverbial. Some of O'Connell's friends, however, thought that he could beat her at the use of her own weapons. Of this, however, he had some doubts himself, when he had listened once or twice to some minor specimens of her Billingsgate. It was mooted once, whether the young Kerry barrister could encounter her, and some one of the company (in O'Connell's presence) rather too freely ridiculed the idea of his being able to meet the famous Madam Moriarty. O'Connell never liked the idea of being put down, and he professed his readiness to encounter her, and even backed himself for the match. Bets were offered and taken—it was decided that the match should come off at once.

The party adjourned to the huckster's stall, and there was the owner herself, superintending the sale of her small wares—a few loungers and ragged idlers were hanging round her stall—for Biddy was 'a character,' and, in her way, was one of the sights of Dublin.

O'Connell was very confident of success. He had laid an ingenious plan for overcoming her, and, with all the anxiety of an ardent experimentalist, waited to put it into practice. He resolved to open the attack. At this time O'Connell's own party, and the loungers about the place, formed an audience quite sufficient to rouse Mrs. Moriarty, on public provocation, to a due exhibition of her powers. O'Connell commenced the attack:—

"What's the price of this walking-stick, Mrs. What's-your-Name?"

"Moriarty, sir, is my name, and a good one it is; and what have you to say agen it? and one-and-sixpence's the price of the stick. Troth, it's chape as dirt—so it is."

"One-and-sixpence for a walking-stick? whew! why, you are know no better than an impostor, to ask eighteen pence for what cost you twopence."

"Twopence, your grandmother!" replied Mrs.

Biddy: "do you mane to say that it's chating the people I am?—impostor, indeed!"

"Aye, impostor; and it's that I call you to your teeth," rejoined O'Connell.

"Come cut your stick, you cantankerous jackanapes."

"Keep a civil tongue in your head, you old *diagonal*," cried O'Connell, calmly.

"Stop your jaw, you pug-nosed badger, or by this and that," cried Mrs. Moriarty, "I'll make you go quicker nor you came."

"Don't be in a passion, my old *radius*—anger will only wrinkle your beauty."

"By the hokey, if you say another word of impudence I'll tan your dirty hide, you bastely common scrub; and sorry I'd be to soil my fists upon your carcase."

"Whew! boys, what a passion old Biddy is in; I protest, as I'm a gentleman——"

"Jintleman! jintleman! the likes of you a jintleman! Wisha, by gor, that bangs Banagher. Why, you potato-faced pippin-sneezer, when did a Madagascar monkey like you pick enough of common Christian dacency to hide your Kerry brogue?"

"Easy, now—easy, now," cried O'Connell, with imperturbable good humor, "don't choke yourself with fine language, you old whiskey-drinking *parallelogram.*"

"What's that you call me, you murderin' villian?" roared Mrs. Moriarty, stung to fury.

"I call you," answered O'Connell, "a parallelogram; and a Dublin judge and jury will say that it's no libel to call you so!"

"Oh, tare-an-ouns! oh, holy Biddy! that on honest woman like me should be called a parry-bellygrum to her face. I'm none of your parry-bellygrums, you rascally gallowsbird; you cowardly, sneaking, plate-lickin' bliggard!"

"Oh, not you, indeed!" retorted O'Connell; "why, I suppose you'll deny that you keep a *hypothenuse* in your house."

"It's a lie for you, you dirty robber, I never had such a thing in my house, you swindling thief."

"Why, sure your neighbors all know very well that you keep not only a hypothenuse, but that you have two *diameters* locked up in your garret, and that you go out to walk with them every Sunday, you heartless old *heptagon.*"

"Oh, hear that, ye saints in glory! Oh, there's

bad language from a fellow that wants to pass for a jintleman. May the divil fly away with you, you micher from Munster, and make celery-sauce of your rotten limbs, you mealy-mouthed tub of guts."

"Ah, you can't deny the charge, you miserable *submultiple* of a *duplicate ratio*."

"Go, rinse your mouth in the Liffey, you nasty tickle pitcher; after all the bad words you speak, it ought to be filthier than your face, you dirty chicken of Beelzebub."

"Rinse your own mouth, you wicked-minded old *polygon*—to the deuce I pitch you, you blustering intersection of a stinking *superficies!*"

"You saucy tinker's apprentice, if you don't cease your jaw, I'll——" But here she gasped for breath, unable to hawk up any more words, for the last volley of O'Connell had nearly knocked the wind out of her.

"While I have a tongue I'll abuse you, you most inimitable *periphery*. Look at her, boys! there she stands—a convicted *perpendicular* in petticoats. There's contamination in her *circumference*, and she trembles with guilt down to the extremities of her *corollaries*. Ah! you're found out, you *rectilineal antecedent,* and *equiangular* old hag! 'Tis with you the devil will fly away, you porter-swiping *similitude* of the *bisection of a vortex!*"

Overwhelmed with this torrent of language, Mrs. Moriarty was silenced. Catching up a saucepan, she was aiming at O'Connell's head, when he very prudently made a timely retreat.

"You have won the wager, O'Connell—here's your bet," cried the gentleman who proposed the contest.

O'Connell knew well the use of sound in the vituperation, and having to deal with an ignorant scold, determined to overcome her in volubility, by using all the *sesquipedalia verba* which occur in Euclid. With these, and a few significant epithets, and a scoffing, impudent demeanor, he had for once imposed silence on Biddy Moriarty.

O'CONNELL AND A BILKING CLIENT.

He used to lodge, when at Cork, at a stationer's of the name of O'Hara, in Patrick-street, one of the principal thoroughfares of the city. There, during the Assizes, there was always a crowd before his door, lounging under his windows, anxious to get a peep at the Counsellor. Whenever he made his appearance there was always a hearty cheer. On one occasion, an old friend of his, who had once belonged to the bar, Mr. K——, a member of a most respectable family, called on O'Connell during the Assizes, to pay him a friendly visit. He found O'Connell engaged with a shrewd-looking farmer, who was consulting him on a knotty case. Heartily glad to see his old friend, O'Connell sprang forward, saying, "My dear K——, I'm delighted to see you." The farmer, seeing the visitor come in, cunningly took the opportunity of sneaking away. He had got what he wanted—the opinion; but O'Connell had not got what *he* wanted—the fee. O'Connell at once followed the farmer, who had got the start by a flight of stairs. The rustic quickened his pace when he found that the counsellor was in chase. O'Connell saw that he could not catch the runaway client, who was now on the flight leading into the hall. He leant over the bannister, and made a grasp at the farmer's collar, but, instead of the collar, he caught the rustic's wig, which came away in his hand. O'Connell gave a shout of laughter, and, quick as thought, jumped in high spirits back to his room. "Hurrah! see, K——, I've got the rascal's wig." Up went the window—

"Three cheers for the counsellor!—Long life to your honor. Arrah! isn't he the man of the people."

"Ah! boys," said O'Connell, with glee, "look here what I've got for you! Here's the wig of a rascal that has just bilked me of a fee."

Shouts of laughter rent the air, as the wig was pitched out, to undergo a rapid process of radical reform at the hands of the mob. As the wigless farmer made his appearance, he was received with groans of derision, and was glad enough to escape with unbroken bones.

SOW-WEST AND THE WIGS.

The following humorous scene took place in the Court-house, Green-street, Dublin:

The city of Dublin was often contested by Mr. John B. West—a conservative barrister of no ordinary talents, whose early end caused much regret. That gentleman was very heavy and clumsy in appearance, and moved very awkwardly. Lord Plunket humorously called him

Sow-West, a name that adhered to him most tenaciously. O'Connell was opposed to West on three or four different occasions. It is remarkable that the opening scenes at the Dublin elections are conducted with far more decorum than similar scenes in other parts of Ireland. All the masses are not admitted indiscriminately to the Court where the hustings are placed—the people are admitted by tickets, half of which are allotted to each rival party. It is the interest of both parties to keep order, and the candidates and their friends are therefore heard with tolerable fairness. On the first day of a Dublin election, the most eloquent members of either party come forward to uphold their favorite principles.

On the occasion referred to, O'Connell, in addressing the people, referred to the appearance of *Sow*-West, whom he humorously quizzed upon the beauty of his appearance.

In reply Mr West said, "Ah, my friends! it's all very well for Mr O'Connell to attack me upon my appearance; but I can tell you, if you saw Mr. O'Connell without his wig, he does not present a face which is much to boast of."

To the surprise of the spectators, no less than

of Mr. West himself, O'Connell walked across, pulled off his wig, stood close by West, and cried out—"There, now, which of us is the better-looking—my wig is off."

This sally of practical humor was received with bursts of laughter and cheering. O'Connell looked admirably, exhibiting a skull which, for volume and development, was not to be surpassed."

ELECTION AND RAILWAY DINNERS.

O'Connell's enormous appetite often excited surprise. He ate a prodigious quantity, even for a man of such large frame. At one of the Irish elections, he was greatly annoyed at his candidate being unseated for a few months, by the blundering decision of the assessor. On the day when the election terminated, O'Connell was engaged to dine with a Roman Catholic priest, who piqued himself not a little on the honor of entertaining the Liberator. The company assembled at the appointed hour, much dispirited at the adverse turn which the election had taken at the last moment. O'Connell himself was particularly angry, and chafed with ill-temper at the blunder of the assessor, who would not even listen to his arguments.

Dinner came on, and a turkey-pout smoked before the hospitable clergyman. "Mr. O'Connell, what part of the fowl shall I help you to?" cried the reverend host, with an air of *empressement.*

His ears were electrified by O'Connell's rejoinder—"Oh! hang it, cut it through the middle, and give me half the bird!"

For an orator of a style so copious and diffuse, it was singular how admirably laconic he could become when he chose. During dinner, while occupied with the viands, he would express himself with the terseness and condensation of Tacitus.

A railway company once gave a complimentary dinner at Kingstown, and O'Connell, who had supported the Bill in the House of Commons, was invited. The sea breeze on the Kingstown pier sharpened his appetite. He had already partaken heartily of the second course, when one of the directors, seeing O'Connell's plate nearly empty, asked—"Pray, sir, what will you be helped to *next?*"

Hastily glancing at the dishes still untasted,

O'Connell, with a full mouth, answered—"Mutton—well done—and much of it."

SCENE AT KILLINEY.

O'Connell was a capital actor, and his dramatic delivery of a common remark was often highly impressive. Many years since, he went down to Kingstown, near Dublin, with a party, to visit a queen's ship-of-war, which was then riding in the bay.

After having seen it, O'Connell proposed a walk to the top of Killiney Hill. Breaking from the rest of his party, he ascended to the highest point of the hill, in company with a young and real Irish patriot, whose character was brimful of national enthusiasm. The day was fine, and the view from the summit of the hill burst gloriously upon the sight. The beautiful bay of Dublin, like a vast sheet of crystal, was at their feet. The old city of Dublin stretched away to the west, and to the north was the old promontory of Howth, jutting forth into the sea. To the south were the Dublin and Wicklow mountains, enclosing the lovely vale of Shanganah, rising picturesquely against the horizon. The scene was beautiful, with all the varieties of sunlight and shadow.

O'Connell enjoyed it with nearly as much rapture as his youthful and ardent companion, who broke forth—"It is all Ireland—oh! how beautiful! Thank God, we see nothing English here. Everything we see is Irish!"

His rapture was interrupted by O'Connell, gently laying his hand on his shoulder, and pointing to the ship-of-war at anchor, as he exclaimed—"*A speck of the British power!*"

The thought was electric. That speck, significantly pointed out by O'Connell, suggested the whole painful history of his fatherland to the memory of the ardent young Irishman.

AN INSOLENT JUDGE.

The judges themselves often came in for a share of his animadversions, when he deemed their judicial or other conduct deserved public censure; and when he pleaded as an advocate before them, their resentment betrayed itself. Singular to say, his practice was never injuriously affected by his boldness outside. Other men have suffered vitally from the political or personal hostility of judges

—Curran was one of them. But O'Connell beat down the most formidable hatred, and compelled, by the sheer force of legal and intellectual power, the bitterest and most obstinate personal rancor to give way. He compelled pompous, despotic, and hostile judges to yield. He could not be awed. If they were haughty, he was proud. If they were malevolent, he was cuttingly sarcastic.

It happened that he was by at an argument in one of the courts of Dublin, in the course of which a young Kerry attorney was called upon by the opposing counsel, either to admit a statement as evidence, or to hand in some documents he could legally detain. O'Connell was not specially engaged. The discussion arose on a new trial motion—the issue to go down to the Assizes. He did not interfere until the demand was made on the attorney, but he then stood up and told him to make no admission.

He was about to resume his seat, when the judge, Baron M'Cleland, said, with a peculiar emphasis, "Mr. O'Connell, have you a *brief* in this case?"

"No, my lord, I have not; but I *will* have one, when the case goes down to the Assizes."

"When *I*," rejoined the judge, throwing himself back with an air of lofty scorn, "was at the bar, it was not *my* habit to anticipate briefs."

"When *you* were at the bar," retorted O'Connell, "*I* never chose *you* for a model; and now that you are on the Bench, I shall not submit to your dictation." Leaving his lordship to digest the retort, he took the attorney by the arm, and walked him out of Court. In this way he dealt with hostile judges.

A WITNESS CAJOLED.

O'Connell knew so intimately the habits and character of the humbler class, that he was able, by cajolery or intimidation, to coerce them, when on the table, into truth-telling. He was once examining a witness, whose inebriety, at the time to which the evidence referred, it was essential to his client's case to prove. He quickly discovered the man's character. He was a fellow who may be discribed as "half foolish with roguery."

"Well, Darby," said the Counsellor, taking him on the cross-examination, "you told the whole truth to that gentleman?" pointing to the counsel who had just examined the witness.

"Yes, your honor, Counsellor O'Connell."

"How, do you know my name?"

"Ah, sure every one knows our own *pathriot*."

"Well, you are a good-humored, honest fellow Now, tell me, Darby, did you take a drop of anything that day?"

"Why, your honor, I took my share of a pint of spirits."

"Your share of it; now by virtue of your oath, was not your share of it *all but the pewter?*"

"Why, then, dear knows, that's true for you, sir."

The Court was convulsed at both question and answer. It soon came out that the man was drunk, and was not, therefore, a competent witness. Thus O'Connell won the case for his client.

HIS DUEL WITH CAPTAIN D'ESTERRE.

When O'Connell found the Government determined to strain the Convention Act to the utmost, and not permit the existence of any delegated committee for the management of Catholic affairs, he issued circulars to a number of gentlemen to meet him, as individuals, in Capel-street. From that circular arose the Catholic Association.

It was at one of the early meetings of this body that he called the municipal functionaries of Dublin, "a beggarly Corporation." He had become exceedingly obnoxious to the Orange party. He was an object of intense hatred within the precincts of the Castle. To get rid of such a man would be an invaluable service. The *insult* he had put on the *immaculate* and *wealthy* Corporation, offered too inviting an opportunity to be passed over. A champion of Ascendancy appeared in the person of Captain D'Esterre.

On the 1st of February, 1815, nearly eleven days after the insult was received, and eight days after explanation was demanded and refused, this misled gentleman was advised to send a message. He addressed a letter in the following words:—

"Sir—*Carrick's Paper*, of the 23rd instant, in its Report of the Debates of a Meeting of the Catholic Gentlemen, on the subject of a Petition, states that you applied the appellation of *Beggarly*, to the Corporation of this City, *calling it a beggarly Corporation*; and, therefore, as a member of that body, and feeling how painful such is, I beg leave to inquire whether you really used or expressed yourself in such language.

"I feel the more justified in calling on you on this occasion, as such language was not warranted or provoked by any thing on the part of the Corporation; neither was it consistent with the subject of your Debate, or the deportment of the other Catholic gentlemen, who were present; and, though I view it so inconsistent in every respect, I am in hopes the Editor is under error, not you.

"I have further to request your reply in the course of the evening—and remain, Sir, your obedient servant,

"J. N. D'ESTERRE,

"11 Bachelor's-walk, 26th Jan. 1815.

"To Counsellor O'Connell, Merrion-square."

"Sir—In reply to your letter of yesterday, and without either admitting or disclaiming the expression respecting the Corporation of Dublin, in the print to which you allude, I deem it right to inform you, that, from the calumnious manner in which the religion and character of the Catholics of Ireland are treated in that body, no terms attributed to me, however reproachful, can exceed the contemptuous feelings I entertain for that body in its corporate capacity—although, doubtless, it contains many valuable persons, whose conduct, as individuals (I lament), must necessarily be confounded in the acts of the general body.

"I have only to add, *that this Letter must close our Correspondence on this subject.*—I am, &c., &c.,

"DANIEL O'CONNELL.

"Merrion-square, January 27, 1815.

"To J. N. D'Esterre, Esq.,
11 Bachelor's-walk, Dublin."

Mr. D'Esterre was advised to persist in the correspondence, and addressed another letter (but directed in a different hand-writing), to Mr. O'Connell. It was returned to him by Mr. James O'Connell, inclosed in a letter couched in the following terms:—

"Sir—From the tenor of your letter of yesterday, my brother did not expect that your next communication would have been made in *writing.* He directed me to open his letters in his absence; your last letter, bearing a different address from the former one, was opened by me; but upon perceiving the name subscribed, I have declined to read it; and by his directions I return it to you inclosed, and *unread.*—I am, sir, your obedient servant,

"JAMES O'CONNELL.

"Merrion-square, Friday Evening.

"To J. N. D'Esterre, Esq.,
11 Bachelor's-walk.

After a number of insulting letters from D'Esterre, his long-expected hostile message arrived.

Major M'Namara, of Doolen, having been commmissioned by O'Connell, proceeded to Sir Edward Stanley, who acted as the friend of D'Esterre, to arrange the meeting. The hour appointed was three o'clock on Wednesday; the place, Bishop's Court Demesne, Lord Ponsonby's seat, in the county Kildare, thirteen miles distant from Dublin.

It was proposed by him that the mode of fighting should be after the following fashion:—That both should be handed a brace of pistols; reserve their shots until the signal, and then fire when they pleased; advancing or retiring after each shot, as they thought proper. Major M'Namara would not assent to this mode of fighting, without first consulting O'Connell and his friends. O'Connell at once directed him to accept the terms. Major M'Namara then returned to Sir Edward Stanley, and finally arranged the meeting. The parties proceeded to take their ground, and were handed a brace of pistols each. The signal was given. Both reserved their fire for some moments. D'Esterre first changed his position, moving a pace towards the left hand, and then stepped towards O'Connell. His object was to induce him to fire, more or less, at random. He lifted his pistol, as if about to fire. O'Connell instantly presented, pulled the trigger, and the unfortunate man fell.

In close attendance on O'Connell, at the ground, were Major M'Namara, Nicholas Purcell O'Gorman, and Richard Nugent Bennett, as seconds and friends; for all may be said to have acted in the double capacity.

It was reported in Dublin that O'Connell was shot; and a party of dragoons were despatched from Dublin, for the protection of D'Esterre. On their way the officer by whom they were commanded met, on its return, the carriage containing O'Connell and his brother. The officer called on the postilion to stop; whereupon Mr. James O'Connell pulled down the window. The officer, addressing him, asked if they had been present at the duel, to which he replied in the affirmative. The officer then said, "Is it true Mr. O'Connell has been shot?" Mr. James O'Connell replied, "No; the reverse is the fact; Mr. D'Esterre has unfortunately fallen." The announcement had a visible effect upon the military; they were not prepared for the intelligence; and something like consternation was exhibited. The carriage was allowed to proceed, the military party being evidently not aware who were its occupants.

When D'Esterre fell the spectators present could not refrain from giving expression to their excited feelings; they actually shouted; and a young collegian who was present, and who became a Protestant clergyman, was so carried away by the general feeling, as to fling up his hat in the air, and shout, "Hurra for O'Connell!"

Very different was the conduct of the three occupants of O'Connell's carriage. They displayed no exultation. The moment D'Esterre fell they went off; and though the place of meeting was near Naas, they were close to Dublin before a single word was exchanged between them. At last O'Connell broke the silence, saying, "I fear he is dead, he fell so suddenly. Where do you think he was hit?" "In the head, I think," said his medical friend. "That cannot be—I aimed low; the ball must have entered near the thigh." This will be considered a remarkable observation when, as was subsequently found, the wound was inflicted in the part mentioned by O'Connell. Being one of the surest shots that ever fired a pistol, he could have hit his antagonist where he pleased. But his object was merely, in self-defence, to wound him in no mortal part, and he aimed low with that intention.

The excitement in Dublin, when the result was known, cannot be described; and, indeed, is scarcely credited by those who were not then in the metropolis. Over seven hundred gentlemen left their cards at O'Connell's the day after the occurrence.

Great commiseration was felt for D'Esterre's family, but it was considered that he himself lost his life foolishly. It may be added that he was an officer in the navy, and an eccentric character. He at one time played off rather a serious joke upon his friends, who resided near Cork. He wrote to them from aboard that he was sentenced to be hanged for mutiny, and implored of them to use every interest to save him. Lord Shannon interested himself in the affair, and the greatest trouble was taken to obtain a pardon. But it turned out to be a hoax practised by D'Esterre, when under the influence of the Jolly God. Knowing his character, many even of opposite politics, notwithstanding the party spirit that then prevailed, regretted the issue the unfortunate man provoked.

O'CONNELL AND SECRETARY GOULBURN.

Mr. Goulburn, while Secretary for Ireland, visited Killarney, when O'Connell (then on circuit) happened to be there. Both stopped at Finn's Hotel, and chanced to get bedrooms opening off the same corridor. The early habits of O'Connell made him be up at cock-crow. Finding the hall-door locked, and so being hindered from walking outside, he commenced walking up and down the corridor. To pass the time, he repeated aloud some of Moore's poetry, and had just uttered the lines—

"We tread the land that bore us,
The green flag flutters o'ers us,
The friends we've tried are by our side—

At this moment Goulburn popped his nightcapped head out, to see what was the matter. O'Connell instantly pointed his finger at him, and finished the verse—

And the foe we hate before us!"

In went Goulburn's head in the greatest hurry.

ENTRAPPING A WITNESS.

An illustration of his dexterity in compassing an unfortunate culprit's acquittal may be here narrated.

He was employed in defending a prisoner who was tried for a murder committed in the vicinity of Cork. The principal witness swore strongly against the prisoner—one corroborative circumstance was, that the prisoner's hat was found near the place where the murder took place. The witness swore positively the hat produced was the one found, and that it belonged to the prisoner, whose name was James.

"By virtue of your oath, are you positive that

this is the same hat?" "Yes." "Did you examine it carefully before you swore in your informations that it was the prisoner's?" Yes." "Now, let me see," said O'Connell, and he took up the hat, and began carefully to examine the inside. He then spelled aloud the name James—slowly, thus: —"J—a—m—e—s." "Now, do you mean those words were in the hat when you found it?" "I do." "Did you see them there." "I did." "This is the same hat?" "It is." "Now, my Lord," said O'Connell, holding up the hat to the Bench, "there is an end to the case—there is no name whatever inscribed in the hat." The result was instant acquittal.

GAINING OVER A JURY.

At a Cork Assizes, many years ago, he was employed in an action of damages, for diverting a stream from its regular channel, or diverting so much of it as inflicted injury on some party who previously benefited by its abundance. The injury was offered by a nobleman, and his attorney, on whose advice the proceeding was adopted, was a man of corpulent proportions, with a face bearing the ruddy glow of rude health, but, flushed in a crowded court, assumed momentarily, a color like that imparted by intemperance. He really was a most temperate man.

O'Connell dwelt on the damage his client had sustained by the unjust usurpation. The stream should have been permitted to follow its old and natural course. There was neither law nor justice in turning it aside from his client's fields. He had a right to all its copiousness, and the other party should have allowed him full enjoyment. In place of that, the latter monopolized the water—he diminished it. It became every day small by degrees and beautifully less. "There is not now," he said, "gentlemen of the jury, a tenth of the ordinary quantity. The stream is running dry—and so low is it, and so little of it is there, that," continued he, turning to the rubicund attorney, and naming him, "there isn't enough in it to make grog for Fogarty."

A roar of laughter followed, and it was not stopped by the increased rosiness and embarrassment of the gentleman who became the victim of the learned advocate's humorous allusion. The tact in this sally was, in endeavoring to create an impression on the jury that his poor client was sacrificed by the harsh conduct of a grog-drinking attorney, and thus create prejudice against the plaintiff's case. Thus did O'Connell gain the hearts of Irish juries; and thus did he, indulging his own natural humor, on the public platform, gain the affections of his countrymen.

PADDY AND THE PARSON.

In June, 1832, O'Connell addressed a meeting of the Political Union of the London working classes. In his address, he humorously and graphically describes the system of passive resistance then adopted against the payment of Tithes, in the following amusing dialogue between Paddy and the parson:—

"And how does Paddy act? Does he disobey the laws? No. 'Paddy,' says the parson, 'you owe me £1 17s. 6d.' 'And what may it be for, your Riverence?' says Pat (laughter). 'Tithes! Paddy.' 'Arrah! thin I suppose your Riverence gave some value fornint I was born; for divil a bit I ever seen since (roars of laughter). But your Riverence, I suppose, has law for it? Bless the law! your honor, and sure an I wouldn't be after going to disobey it; but plase your Riverence, I have no money' (great laughter). 'Ah, Pat, but you've a cow there. 'Yes, your Riverence, that's the cow that gives food to Norry and the fourteen childer.' 'Well, Paddy, then I must distrain that cow.' 'If your honor has law for it, to be sure you will.' Well, what does Paddy do? He stamps the word 'Tithes' upon her side, and the parson can't find a soul to take the cow. So he gets a regiment and a half, by way of brokers (much laughter)—fourteen or fifteen companies, with those amiable young gentlemen, their officers, at their head, who march seventeen or eighteen miles across the Bog of Allen to take his cow; they bring the cow to Carlow; when they get there, they find a great crowd assembled; the parson rubs his hands with glee. 'Plenty of customers for the cow,' quoth he to himself. The cow is put up at £2—no bidder; £1—no bidder; 10*s*—5*s*.—6*d*.—1½*d*. (cheers). Not a soul will bid, and back goes the cow to Norry and the fourteen childer (continued cheers)."

A MARTIAL JUDGE.

In Court his usual mirth and ready wit never

failed him; and he kept the bar and listening by-standers in constant hilarity. He made an excellent hit during the trial of Sir George Bingham, for assault, during the tithe agitation. The General's Aide-de-Camp, Captain Berners, of the Royal Artillery, was under examination. A junior counsel asked the witness, "What is the meaning of the military phrase, 'ride him down?'"

"Do you think" interposed O'Connell, "we are here to get an explanation of plain English from an English Aide-de-Camp, with his tongue in holiday dress?" then turning to the witness, he said, "You belong to the Artillery and understand horse language?"—"Yes." Mr. Justice Moore, who tried the case, here observed—'I ought to understand it, Mr. O'Connell, for I was a long while Captain of cavalry." "Yes you were, my lord," replied O'Connell, "and I recollect you a long time a *Sergeant*, too." This ready sally caused a burst of laughter throughout the whole court.

RETENTIVE MEMORY.

At Darrynane, he was sitting one morning, surrounded by country people, some asking his advice, some his assistance, others making their grievances known. Amongst the rest was a farmer rather advanced in life, a swaggering sort of fellow, who was desirous to carry his point by impressing the Liberator with the idea of his peculiar honesty and respectability. He was anxious that O'Connell should decide a matter in dispute between him and a neighboring farmer who, he wished to insinuate, was not as good as he ought to be. "For my part, I, at least, can boast that neither I nor mine were ever brought before a judge or sent to jail, however it was with others."

"Stop, stop, my fine fellow," cried the Liberator—"Let me see," pausing a moment. "Let me see; it is now just twenty-five years ago, last August, that I myself saved you from transportation, and had you discharged from the dock."

The man was thunderstruck; he thought such a matter could not be retained in the great man's mind. He shrunk away, murmuring that he should get justice elsewhere, and never appeared before the Liberator afterwards.

A POLITICAL HURRAH AT A FUNERAL.

Ascending the mountain road between Dublin and Glencullen, in company with an English friend, O'Connell was met by a funeral. The mourners soon recognized him, and immediately broke into a vociferous hurrah for their political favorite, much to the astonishment of the Sassenach; who, accustomed to the solemn and lugubrious decorum of English funerals, was not prepared for an outburst of Celtic enthusiasm upon such an occasion. A remark being made on the oddity of a political hurrah at a funeral, it was replied that the corpse would have doubtless cheered lustily too, if he could.

REFUSAL OF OFFICE.

In 1838, on the morning when O'Connell received from the Government the offer to be appointed Lord Chief Baron, he walked over to the window, saying:

"This is very kind—very kind, indeed!—but I haven't the least notion of taking the offer. Ireland could not spare me now; not but that, *if she could*, I don't at all deny that the office would have great attractions for me. Let me see, now —there would not be more than about eight days' duty in the year; I would take a country house near Dublin, and walk into town; and during the intervals of judicial labor, I'd go to Derrynane. I should be idle in the early part of April, just when the jack-hares leave the most splendid trails upon the mountains. In fact, I should enjoy the office exceedingly upon every account, if I could but accept it consistently with the interests of Ireland—BUT I CANNOT."

A MISTAKEN FRENCHMAN.

When travelling in France, during the time of his sojourn at St. Omer's, O'Connell encountered a very talkative Frenchman, who incessantly poured forth the most bitter tirades against England. O'Connell listened in silence; and the Frenchman, surprised at his indifference, at last exclaimed,—

"Do you hear, do you understand what I am saying, sir?"

"Yes, I hear you, I comprehend you perfectly."

"Yet you do not seem angry?"

"Not in the least."

"How can you so tamely bear the censures I pronounce against your country?"

"Sir, England is not my country. Censure her as much as you please, you cannot offend me. I am an Irishman, and my countrymen have as little reason to love England as yours have, perhaps less."

EPISTOLARY BORES.

The number of letters received by O'Connell upon trivial subjects was sufficient to try his patience, as the following will show:—

A letter once arrived from New York, which, on opening, he found to contain a minute description of a Queen Anne's farthing recently found by the writer, with a modest request that "Ireland's Liberator" might negotiate the sale of the said farthing in London; where, as many intelligent persons had assured him, he might make his fortune by it.

Another modest correspondent was one Peter Waldron, also of New York, whose epistle ran thus:—"Sir, I have discovered an old paper, by which I find that my grandfather, Peter Waldron, left Dublin about the year 1730. You will very much oblige me by instituting an immediate inquiry who the said Peter Waldron was; whether he possessed any property in Dublin or elsewhere, and to what amount; and in case that he did, you will confer a particular favor on me by taking immediate steps to recover it, and if successful, forwarding the amount to me at New York."

At another time a Protestant clergyman wrote to apprise him that he and his family were all in prayer for his conversion to the Protestant religion; and that the writer was anxious to engage in controversy with so distinguished an antagonist.

The letters with which he was persecuted, soliciting patronage, were innumerable. "Everybody writes to me about everything," said he, "and the applicants for places, without a single exception, tell me that *one word* of mine will infallibly get them what they want. *One word!* Oh, how sick I am of that '*One word!*'"

Some of his rural correspondents entertained odd ideas of his attributes. He said that "from one of them he got a letter commencing with 'Awful Sir!'"

SIR R. PEEL'S OPINION OF O'CONNELL.

Sir Robert Peel is said to have expressed his high appreciation of O'Connell's parliamentary abilities. While the Reform Bill was under discussion, the speeches of its friends and foes were one day canvassed at Lady Beauchamp's. On O'Connell's name being mentioned, some critic fastidiously said, "Oh, a broguing Irish fellow! who would listen to *him?* I always walk out of the House when he opens his lips." "Come, Peel," said Lord Westmoreland, "let me hear your opinion." "My opinion candidly is," replied Sir Robert, "that if I wanted an efficient and eloquent advocate, I would readily give up all the other orators of whom we have been talking, provided I had with me this same 'broguing Irish fellow.'"

At the Bishop of Waterford's table, the following anecdote was related by O'Connell:

"My grandmother had twenty-two children, and half of them lived beyond the age of ninety. Old Mr. O'Connell of Derrynane, pitched upon an oak tree to make his own coffin, and mentioned his purpose to a carpenter. In the evening, the butler entered after dinner to say that the carpenter wanted to speak with him. 'For what?' asked my uncle. 'To talk about your honor's coffin,' said the carpenter, putting his head inside the door over the butler's shoulder. I wanted to get the fellow out, but my uncle said, 'Oh! let him in by all means.—Well, friend, what do you want to say to me about my coffin?' 'Only, sir, that I'll saw up the oak tree that your honor was speaking of into seven-foot plank.' 'That would be wasteful,' answered my uncle; 'I never was more than six feet and an inch in my vamps, the best day ever I saw.' 'But your honor will stretch after death,' said the carpenter. 'Not eleven inches, I am sure, you blockhead! But I'll stretch, no doubt—perhaps a couple of inches or so. Well, make my coffin six feet six, and I'll warrant that will give me room enough!'"

"I remember," said O'Connell, "being counsel at a special commission in Kerry against a Mr. S——, and having occasion to press him somewhat hard in my speech, he jumped up in the court, and called me 'a purse-proud blockhead.'

I said to him, 'In the first place I have got no purse to be proud of; and, secondly, if I be a blockhead, it is better for you, as I am counsel against you. However, just to save you the trouble of saying so again, I'll administer a slight rebuke'—whereupon I whacked him soundly on the back with the president's cane. Next day he sent me a challenge by William Ponsonby of Crottoe; but very shortly after, he wrote to me to state, that since he had challenged me, he had discovered that my life was inserted in a very valuable lease of his. 'Under these circumstances,' he continued, 'I cannot afford to shoot you, unless, as a precautionary measure, you first insure your life for my benefit. If you do, then heigh for powder and ball! I'm your man.' Now this seems so ludicrously absurd, that it is almost incredible; yet it is literally true. S—— was a very timid man; yet he fought six duels—in fact, he fought them all out of pure fear."

www.ingramcontent.com/pod-product-compliance
Lightning Source LLC
LaVergne TN
LVHW050518100826
845148LV00002B/376

* 9 7 8 1 4 2 5 5 2 1 0 6 6 *